At Sylvan, we believe reading is one of life's most important and enriching abilities, and we're glad you've chosen our resources to help your child build these critically important skills. We know that the time you spend with your child reinforcing the lessons learned in school will contribute to his love of reading. This love of reading will translate into academic achievement. A successful reader is ready for the world around him, ready to do research, ready to experience the world of literature, and prepared to make the connections necessary to achieve in school and in life.

We use a research-based, step-by-step process in teaching reading at Sylvan that includes thought-provoking reading selections and activities. As students increase their success as readers they become more confident. With increasing confidence, students build even more success. Our Sylvan workbooks are designed to help you to help your child build the skills and confidence that will contribute to your child's success in school.

Included with your purchase of this workbook is a coupon for a discount at a participating Sylvan center. We hope you will use this coupon to further your child's academic journey. Let us partner with you to support the development of a confident, well prepared, independent learner.

The Sylvan Team

Sylvan Learning Center. Unleash your child's potential here.

No matter how big or small the academic challenge, every child has the ability to learn. But sometimes children need help making it happen. Sylvan believes every child has the potential to do great things. And, we know better than anyone else how to tap into that academic potential so that a child's future really is full of possibilities. Sylvan Learning Center is the place where your child can build and master the learning skills needed to succeed and unlock the potential you know is there.

The proven, personalized approach of our in-center programs deliver unparalleled results that other supplemental education services simply can't match. Your child's achievements will be seen not only in test scores and report cards but outside the classroom as well. And when he starts achieving his full potential, everyone will know it. You will see a new level of confidence come through in everything he does and every interaction he has.

How can Sylvan's personalized in-center approach help your child unleash his potential?

- Starting with our exclusive Sylvan Skills Assessment®, we pinpoint your child's exact academic needs.
- Then we develop a customized learning plan designed to achieve your child's academic goals.
- Through our method of skill mastery, your child will not only learn and master every skill in his personalized plan, he will be truly motivated and inspired to achieve his full potential.

To get started, included with this Sylvan product purchase is $10 off our exclusive Sylvan Skills Assessment®. Simply use this coupon and contact your local Sylvan Learning Center to set up your appointment.

And to learn more about Sylvan and our innovative in-center programs, call 1-800-EDUCATE or visit www.SylvanLearning.com. ***With over 1,000 locations in North America, there is a Sylvan Learning Center near you!***

2nd Grade Vocabulary Puzzles

Published in the United States by Random House, Inc., New York, and in Canada by Random House of Canada Limited, Toronto.

www.tutoring.sylvanlearning.com

Created by Smarterville Productions LLC
Producer: TJ Trochlil McGreevy
Producer & Editorial Direction: The Linguistic Edge
Writer: Margaret Crocker
Cover and Interior Illustrations: Delfin Barral and Duendes del Sur
Layout and Art Direction: SunDried Penguin
Art Manager: Adina Ficano

First Edition

ISBN: 978-0-375-43027-5

Library of Congress Cataloging-in-Publication Data available upon request.

This book is available at special discounts for bulk purchases for sales promotions or premiums. For more information, write to Special Markets/Premium Sales, 1745 Broadway, MD 6-2, New York, New York 10019 or e-mail specialmarkets@randomhouse.com.

PRINTED IN CHINA

10 9 8 7 6 5 4 3 2 1

Contents

Look It Up

Word List

READ the words and their meanings.

ad·jec·tive—AJ-ihk-tihv *noun* a word that describes something, like *pretty* or *blue*

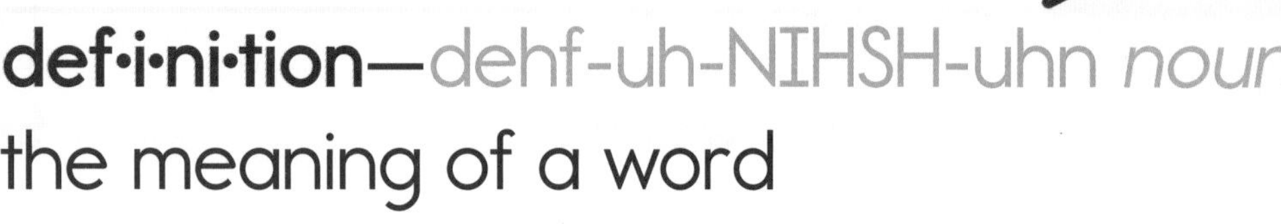

def·i·ni·tion—dehf-uh-NIHSH-uhn *noun* the meaning of a word

de·scribe—dih-SKRIB *verb* to make a picture with words, like "a pretty girl in a blue dress"

dic·tion·ar·y—DIHK-shuh-nehr-ee *noun* a book filled with definitions of words

mean·ing—MEE-nihng *noun* the idea of a word, what it means

noun—nown *noun* a word that stands for a person, place, or thing

verb—verb *noun* a word that stands for an action, like *run*

Match the Meaning

WRITE the words next to their definitions. LOOK at the word box for help.

adjective	definition	dictionary	meaning
noun	~~describe~~	verb	

1. describe ________ to make a word picture
2. ________ the idea of a word
3. ________ an action word
4. ________ a word for a person, place, or thing
5. ________ a word that describes something
6. ________ a book filled with definitions
7. ________ the meaning of a word

ABC-123

Words in a dictionary go in **alphabetical order**. That means words that start with "A" go before words that start with "B."

READ the words in the word box. Then WRITE them in alphabetical order.

machine	octopus	jelly	whisper
balloon	trouble	~~angry~~	learn

1. angry
2. __________
3. __________
4. __________
5. __________
6. __________
7. __________
8. __________

ABCDEFGHIJKLMNOPQRSTUVWXYZ

Pick the One

A **dictionary** tells you whether a word is a *noun*, *adjective*, or *verb*. Those are **parts of speech**.

CIRCLE the correct part of speech for each word.

HINT: If you're not sure, look up the words in a dictionary.

1. **eat**	noun	adjective	verb
2. **purple**	noun	adjective	verb
3. **draw**	noun	adjective	verb
4. **animal**	noun	adjective	verb
5. **young**	noun	adjective	verb
6. **wash**	noun	adjective	verb
7. **tooth**	noun	adjective	verb
8. **stove**	noun	adjective	verb

Dictionary Dare

Guide words are the first and last words on a page in a dictionary. They help you figure out if the word you're looking for is on that page.

READ the guide words. CIRCLE the word in each row that comes between them.

HINT: The words are in alphabetical order. Use the second letter of each word to figure out which word should come in between.

1. **folk → football**	food	frost	find
2. **preschool → president**	peace	puppy	present
3. **trade → train**	tuck	taxi	traffic
4. **robot → roller coaster**	recess	rock	rumble
5. **babble → balloon**	bagpipes	beaver	blob
6. **mold → money**	missile	monarch	mucus
7. **uniform → unlucky**	umpire	useless	unique
8. **haunt → hazy**	hawk	hero	hungry

480 **folk • football**

folk \ˈfōk\ *n. pl* **folk** or **folks** **1** *archaic*: a group of kindr : PEOPLE **2** : the great p determines the g characteristic f

Blank Out

A dictionary also tells you how many syllables a word has. A **syllable** is each part of a word that takes one beat to say. So *mean* has one syllable and *meaning* has two syllables. A dot shows the break for each syllable: *mean•ing.*

READ each word out loud. Then WRITE the number of syllables.

1. ad•jec•tive ____3____
2. def•i•ni•tion ________
3. de•scribe ________
4. dic•tion•ar•y ________
5. mean•ing ________
6. noun ________
7. syl•la•ble ________
8. verb ________

Word List

READ the words and their meanings.

ar•rive—uh-RIV *verb* to come to a place

at•tempt—uh-TEHMPT *verb* to try to do something

beau•ti•ful—BYOO-tuh-fuhl *adjective* very pretty

en•e•my—EHN-uh-mee *noun* someone who is working against you, a foe

fail—fayl *verb* to lose, to not get what you tried for

gi•ant—JI-uhnt 1. *noun* a huge person or other creature out of a fairy tale 2. *adjective* very big

pred•a•tor—PREHD-uh-ter *noun* an animal or insect that hunts others for its food

suc•ceed—suhk-SEED *verb* to win, to get what you wanted

Match the Meaning

WRITE the words next to their definitions. LOOK at the word box for help.

arrive	attempt	beautiful	enemy
fail	giant	predator	succeed

1. ____________________ really large
2. ____________________ to lose
3. ____________________ to win
4. ____________________ a hunter
5. ____________________ to come
6. ____________________ really pretty
7. ____________________ to try
8. ____________________ someone who's out to get you

Pick the One

Some words mean the same thing, like *start* and *begin*. Others are **opposites**, like *night* and *day*.

READ each word pair. CIRCLE "same" if they have the same meaning and "opposite" if the words are opposites.

1. arrive	leave	same	opposite
2. giant	huge	same	opposite
3. fail	succeed	same	opposite
4. beautiful	ugly	same	opposite
5. attempt	try	same	opposite
6. predator	hunter	same	opposite
7. enemy	friend	same	opposite
8. arrive	come	same	opposite

Find the Friend

READ the clues. Then WRITE the friend's name under each picture.

Darla is tall and thin.

Joe has curly black hair.

Kira wears the same shirt as Darla.

Talia is facing the opposite direction.

Larry is the opposite of Darla.

Who am I?

________ 1 ________ 2 ________ 3 ________ 4 ________ 5

Criss Cross

READ the clues. FILL IN the boxes with the right word for each clue.

Across

2. Same as *come*
4. Opposite of *tiny*
5. Opposite of *succeed*

Down

1. Same as *pretty*
3. Opposite of *buddy*

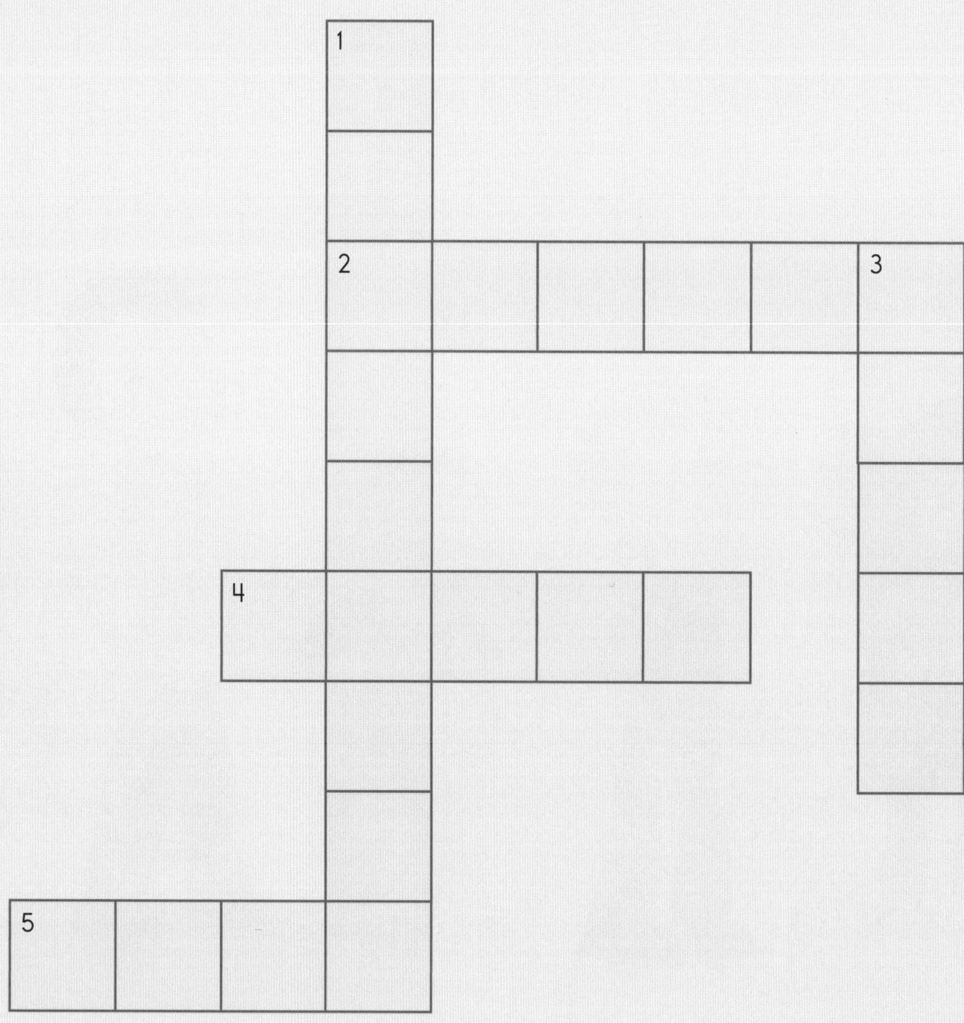

Dictionary Dare

Did you see that the word *giant* had two definitions in the Word List? Some words have more than one meaning. A dictionary gives all the meanings of a word.

READ the definition. Then ANSWER the questions.

skate—skayt 1. *noun* a shoe with a sharp blade that helps you slide on ice 2. *noun* a shoe with wheels that help you roll on the sidewalk 3. *verb* to use skates to move along the ground or on ice

1. How many meanings does *skate* have? __________
2. Is *skate* ever an adjective? Circle one: YES NO
3. Use *skate* in a sentence as a verb. ________________

____

____

____

______________________________.

Word List

READ the words and their meanings.

base•ball—BAYS-bahl 1. *noun* a game played with a bat, a ball, and four bases 2. *noun* a ball used for playing baseball

bath•room—BATH-room *noun* a room for bathing and using the toilet

eve•ry•where—EHV-ree-wehr *adverb* in all places

light•house—LIT-hows *noun* a tall building with a big light that helps boats see the shore

side•walk—SID-wawk *noun* a smooth, hard walkway

stop•light—STAHP-lit *noun* a light that helps move traffic safely where two roads cross

sun•rise—SUHN-riz *noun* the time of day when the sun comes up

tooth•paste—TOOTH-payst *noun* a cream used to clean teeth

Match the Meaning

WRITE the words next to their definitions. LOOK at the word box for help.

baseball	bathroom	everywhere	sunrise
lighthouse	sidewalk	stoplight	toothpaste

1. ____________________ all over the world
2. ____________________ the very beginning of the day
3. ____________________ a game played with a bat
4. ____________________ a walkway
5. ____________________ a guide for ships at sea
6. ____________________ what you use to brush your teeth
7. ____________________ where you find a toilet
8. ____________________ a traffic light at a corner

Finish the Story

READ the story. FILL IN the blanks with words from the word box.

bathroom	baseball	sidewalk	stoplight	sunrise	toothpaste

Just in Time

I got up at _______________ (1) to play _______________ (2) with my pals. As I raced to get ready, I dripped _______________ (3) from my brush onto the floor in the _______________ (4). Mom wasn't up yet, so I didn't clean it. I grabbed my bat and ran down the _______________ (5) to the corner. Luckily the _______________ (6) was green, so I could cross. I got to the park just in time to bat!

Add It Up

Compound words are made by putting two words together.

ADD UP the smaller words to make compound words that match the definitions.

Example: *light + house = lighthouse*
a light that helps keep ships safe

1. **grand** + ____________ = ________________________

your mother's father

2. ____________ + **board** = ________________________

a board with wheels used to roll down the sidewalk

3. ____________ + **ground** = ________________________

a place with slides and swings

4. _________ + ___________ = ________________________

a paper filled with the news of the day

5. **green** + ____________ = ________________________

a building to keep plants warm

Night and Day

DRAW a line to match each word under the moon to its opposite under the sun.

HINT: Don't forget to use a dictionary.

sunrise	nothing
troublemaker	playtime
somebody	sunset
downstairs	daytime
nighttime	sidewalk
everything	upstairs
bedtime	peacemaker
highway	nobody

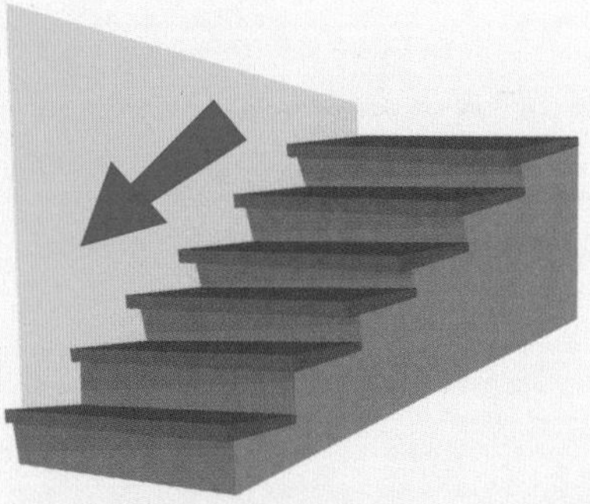

Cross Out

CROSS OUT the words that are NOT compound words.

1. starfish	football	adjective	predator
2. enemy	playground	everybody	arrive
3. lighthouse	beautiful	dictionary	blueberry
4. stoplight	unhappy	nothing	syllable

ABC-123

READ the words in the word box. Then WRITE them in alphabetical order.

dictionary	stoplight	arrive	sidewalk
definition	adjective	attempt	describe

1. ____________________
2. ____________________
3. ____________________
4. ____________________
5. ____________________
6. ____________________
7. ____________________
8. ____________________

ABCDEFGHIJKLMNOPQRSTUVWXYZ

Pick the One

CIRCLE the correct part of speech for each word.

1. **beautiful**	adjective	noun	verb
2. **enemy**	adjective	noun	verb
3. **succeed**	adjective	noun	verb
4. **syllable**	adjective	noun	verb
5. **describe**	adjective	noun	verb
6. **tiny**	adjective	noun	verb
7. **arrive**	adjective	noun	verb
8. **bathroom**	adjective	noun	verb

Same or Opposite?

READ each word pair. CIRCLE if they are the same or opposites.

1. giant	tiny	same	opposite
2. fail	lose	same	opposite
3. beautiful	pretty	same	opposite
4. attempt	quit	same	opposite
5. nap	sleep	same	opposite
6. arrive	come	same	opposite
7. sunrise	sunset	same	opposite
8. everything	nothing	same	opposite

Criss Cross

WRITE the word for each clue in the grid.

adjective describe succeed syllable verb

Across

3. To win
4. An action word

Down

1. To make a word picture
2. A word that describes something
3. One beat of a word

Word List

READ the words and their meanings.

braid—brayd 1. *noun* hair in a rope-like style 2. *verb* to put hair in a rope-like style

cheek—cheek *noun* the side of your face between your nose and your ear. You have two cheeks.

eye·brow—I-brow *noun* the strip of hair above your eye

freck·les—FREHK-lz *noun* spots on skin from the sun

frown—frown 1. *noun* a sad or mad face, the opposite of a smile 2. *verb* to make a sad or mad face

mouth—mowth 1. *noun* the hole in your face where you put your food 2. *verb* to talk with your lips without making a sound

stom·ach—STUHM-uhk *noun* your tummy, or belly, that tells you when you're hungry or full

throat—throht 1. *noun* the front part of your neck 2. *noun* the tube inside your neck that goes to your stomach and your lungs

Match the Meaning

WRITE the words next to their definitions. LOOK at the word box for help.

braid	eyebrow	frown	stomach
cheek	freckles	mouth	throat

1. ____________ the opposite of *smile*
2. ____________ the front of your neck
3. ____________ where your lips and teeth are
4. ____________ a rope-like ponytail
5. ____________ spots on your skin
6. ____________ the strip of hair above your eye
7. ____________ the place where food goes after you put it in your mouth
8. ____________ the side of your face below your eye

Criss Cross

READ the clues. FILL IN the boxes with the right word for each clue.

Across

3. The front of your neck
5. The side of your face

Down

1. The opposite of a smile
2. Your tummy
4. Spots on skin

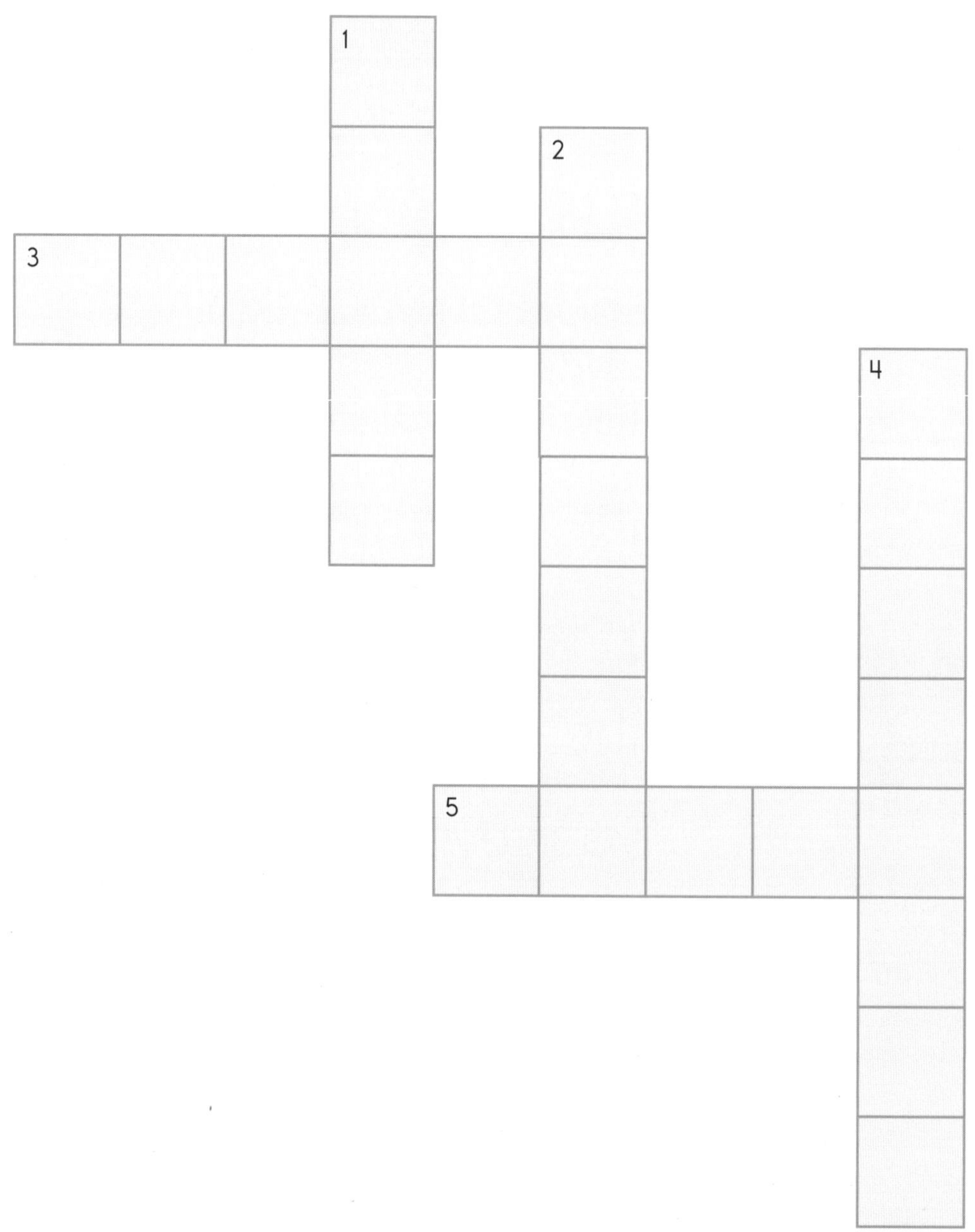

Cross Out

CROSS OUT the words that are **not** parts of the body.

1. finger	throat	verb	definition
2. sunrise	fail	freckles	mouth
3. arm	sidewalk	stomach	attempt
4. syllable	eyebrow	giant	cheek

Find the Friend

READ the clues. Then WRITE the friend's name under each picture.

Doug has freckles on his cheeks.

Carly has two braids.

Tyara is frowning.

Jordan has the biggest eyebrows.

Connor has his mouth open.

Who am I?

______	______	______	______	______
1	2	3	4	5

Blank Out

FILL IN the blanks with the correct words for each part of the picture.

1. ____________________

2. ____________________

3. ____________________

4. ____________________

5. ____________________

6. ____________________

Word List

READ the words and their meanings.

breathe—breeth *verb* to take in air through your mouth or nose

chew—choo *verb* to use your teeth to bite food in your mouth

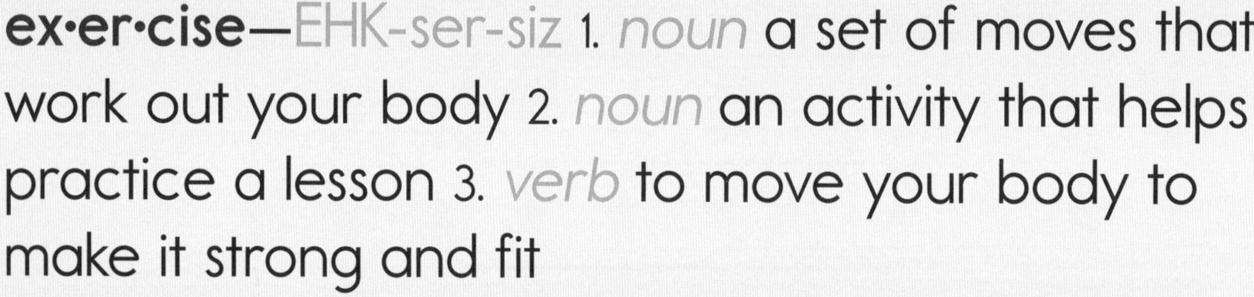

ex•er•cise—EHK-ser-siz 1. *noun* a set of moves that work out your body 2. *noun* an activity that helps practice a lesson 3. *verb* to move your body to make it strong and fit

kneel—neel *verb* to get down on your knees

reach—reech 1. *verb* to put out your hand to get something 2. *verb* to arrive at a place

shiv•er—SHIHV-er 1. *noun* a shake of the body 2. *verb* to shake your body, like when it's cold

squirm—skwerm *verb* to move around in a twisty-turny way

swal•low—SWAHL-oh *verb* to let food go from your mouth into your throat and stomach

Match the Meaning

WRITE the words next to their definitions. LOOK at the word box for help.

breathe	exercise	reach	squirm
chew	kneel	shiver	swallow

1. ____________ to twist and turn
2. ____________ to get down on your knees
3. ____________ to shake
4. ____________ to bite something in your mouth
5. ____________ to put food down your throat
6. ____________ to put out your hand
7. ____________ to suck in air
8. ____________ to help your body stay in shape

Right or Wrong?

UNDERLINE the sentence that matches the picture.

1. 

Maddy is chewing gum.

Maddy is choosing gum.

2. 

Mr. Santos is exiting.

Mr. Santos is exercising.

3.

Ty kicks on the ground.

Ty kneels on the ground.

4.

The baby reaches for her bottle.

The baby reads for her bottle.

Blank Out

FINISH each sentence with a word from the word box.

breathe	exercise	reach	squirming
chew	kneel	shiver	swallow

1. It was so cold out, I started to ________________.
2. Mom goes to the gym to ________________.
3. Ivan is too short to________________ the sink.
4. Aunt Didi always tells me to stop ________________ and sit still.
5. My throat was so sore, it hurt to ________________.
6. I have to ________________ down to look under my bed.
7. If you don't have teeth, how do you ________________?
8. When I get nervous, my mom always tell me, "Just ________________."

Dictionary Dare

LOOK UP the words in a dictionary. Then WRITE the word from the word box that means something similar.

beautiful	chew	reach	squirm
breathe	enemy	shiver	swallow

1. wriggle ____________________
2. inhale ____________________
3. gorgeous ____________________
4. stretch ____________________
5. quake ____________________
6. gulp ____________________
7. gnaw ____________________
8. foe ____________________

Word Pictures

COLOR the spaces that show **verbs**.

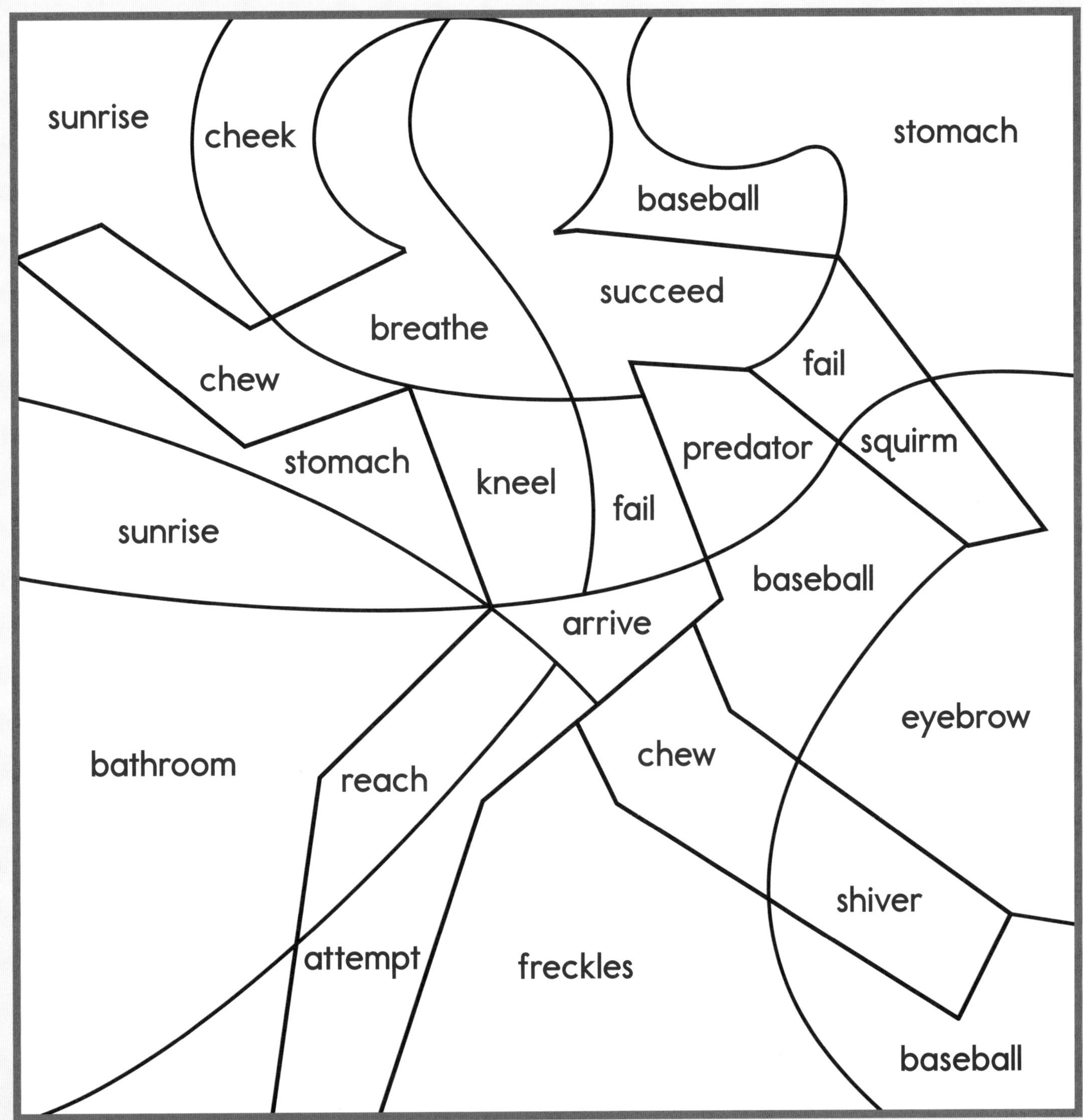

Word List

READ the words and their meanings.

ac•tor—AK-ter *noun* a person who acts on stage or screen

a•dult—uh-DUHLT 1. *noun* a person who is grown up 2. *adjective* fully grown

bar•ber—BAHR-ber *noun* a person who cuts hair

cap•tain—KAP-tihn 1. *noun* the leader of a sports team 2. *noun* the leader of a ship or airplane 3. *noun* the leader of firefighters, police, or the military

crowd—krowd *noun* a lot of people all together

may•or—MAY-er *noun* the leader of a town or city

neigh•bor—NAY-ber *noun* a person who lives next door to or near you

teen—teen *noun* a person who is older than a child but younger than an adult

Match the Meaning

WRITE the words next to their definitions. LOOK at the word box for help.

actor	barber	crowd	neighbor
adult	captain	mayor	teen

1. ____________________ older than a child, but younger than an adult
2. ____________________ someone who is all grown up
3. ____________________ a large group of people
4. ____________________ the star of a movie
5. ____________________ someone who cuts your hair
6. ____________________ the leader of the city
7. ____________________ the head of the team
8. ____________________ a person in the next house

Finish the Story

READ the story. FILL IN the blanks with words from the box.

HINT: Read the whole story before you fill in the blanks.

actor	barber	captain	crowd	mayor	neighbor

Big Game? Big Deal!

Yesterday, I saw a ______ (1) of about one hundred people in front of City Hall. One of them was Mr. Tilcio, the ______ (2) of Folksburg. He gave a big medal to Sara Wells. Sara is the ______ (3) of our soccer team. Mr. Tilcio also gave a medal to Rick Randall, the ______ (4) who stars in Folksburg Follies. But he gave the biggest medal to Mr. Sateen, the ______ (5) who cuts my dad's hair! I couldn't believe it. But my next-door ______ (6) told me that Mr. Sateen saved a baby from a fire. Wow!

Criss Cross

READ the clues. FILL IN the boxes with the right word for each clue.

Across

2. A 15-year-old
4. A grown up
5. A haircutter

Down

1. Someone who lives next door
3. Leader of a town or city

Find the Friend

READ the clues. Then WRITE the friend's name under each picture.

Cyrus is a barber.

Leena is a teen.

Bart is an actor.

Serena is captain of her team.

Hunter is in a crowd.

Who am I?

1 ________ 2 ________ 3 ________ 4 ________ 5 ________

Maze Crazy!

DRAW a line through the words for **people** to help the boy get to the crowd.

Start at the green arrow.

Word List

READ the words and their meanings.

a·gree—uh-GREE 1. *verb* to think the same way as someone else 2. *verb* to say yes to something

bor·row—BAHR-oh *verb* when someone allows you to take something for a short time, then give it back

ex·plain—ihk-SPLAYN *verb* to tell or teach someone about something

for·give—fer-GIHV *verb* to stop being mad and make up after a fight with someone

fright·en—FRIT-uhn *verb* to scare somebody

re·spect—rih-SPEHKT 1. *noun* a feeling that you honor someone 2. *verb* to honor and show consideration for someone

share—shehr 1. *noun* one person's part of something that can be split 2. *verb* to let other people use your things or eat your food 3. *verb* to use something with other people

sug·gest—suhg-JEHST 1. *verb* to hint at something 2. *verb* to give an idea or plan as an option

Match the Meaning

WRITE the words next to their definitions. LOOK at the word box for help.

agree	explain	frighten	share
borrow	forgive	respect	suggest

1. ________________ to honor someone
2. ________________ to let someone use your toys
3. ________________ to check out a book from the library
4. ________________ to make someone understand
5. ________________ to offer an idea
6. ________________ to say yes
7. ________________ to scare someone
8. ________________ to make up and forget a fight

Right or Wrong?

UNDERLINE the sentence that matches the picture.

1.

Tom respects Donna.

Tom does not respect Donna.

2.

Jean shares her pizza with Mike.

Jean won't share her pizza with Mike.

3.

Sondra frightens Neal.

Sondra forgets Neal.

4.

Neal forgives Sondra.

Neal suggests Sondra.

Dictionary Dare

LOOK UP the words in a dictionary. Then WRITE the word from the word box that means the **opposite**.

explain	enemy	agree	respect
beautiful	share	borrow	neighbor

1. loan ____________________
2. confuse ____________________
3. disrespect ____________________
4. hideous ____________________
5. hoard ____________________
6. foreigner ____________________
7. ally ____________________
8. disagree ____________________

Blank Out

FINISH each sentence with a word from the word box.

agree	explain	frighten	shares
borrow	forgive	respect	suggests

1. Miles didn't understand the rules, so I tried to ____________.
2. I will never ____________ Sylvia for calling me a geek!
3. It's important to ____________ the police.
4. Donna ____________ that we play in the tree house today.
5. Mom thinks I should go to bed, but I don't ____________.
6. Taffy never ____________ her popcorn at the movies.
7. Bill tried to ____________ me with his mask, but I wasn't scared.
8. Can I ____________ your video game for a few days?

Cross Out

CROSS OUT the words that are NOT verbs.

1. enemy	beautiful	forgive	attempt
2. frighten	scary	exercise	definition
3. verb	share	throat	borrow
4. respect	sidewalk	suggest	idea

Dictionary Dare

READ the guide words. CIRCLE the word in each row that comes between them.

1. **giggle → girl**	giddy	give	ginger
2. **outline → ovation**	outsmart	outlaw	outcry
3. **spike → spirit**	spindle	spice	spite
4. **attract → author**	auxiliary	aunt	autumn
5. **count → court**	counsel	courtship	country
6. **noon → not**	noise	north	notch
7. **weak → weave**	we	wear	wealth
8. **incline → increase**	incomplete	incense	incite

417 **giggle • girl**

giggle \'gig-əl\ *vb* giggled; gigg
laugh with repeated short c
vt: to utter with a gigg

Match the Meaning

DRAW a line to match the words that mean the same thing.

1. scare	predator
2. succeed	stomach
3. hunter	arrive
4. try	win
5. meaning	frighten
6. come	shiver
7. tummy	definition
8. shake	attempt

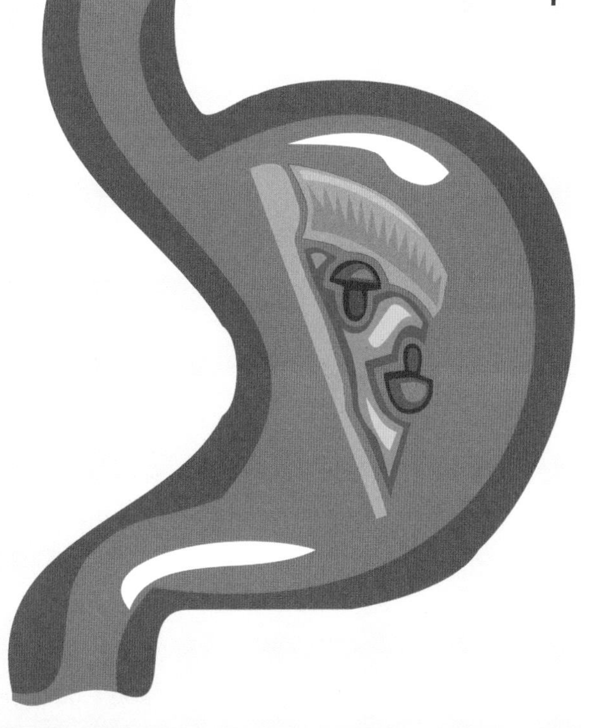

Criss Cross

READ the clues. FILL IN the boxes with the right word for each clue.

chew crowd explain squirm suggest swallow

Across

1. Offer an idea
3. Bite on something
4. Teach or tell something
5. Lots of people

Down

1. Put something down your throat
2. Twist and turn

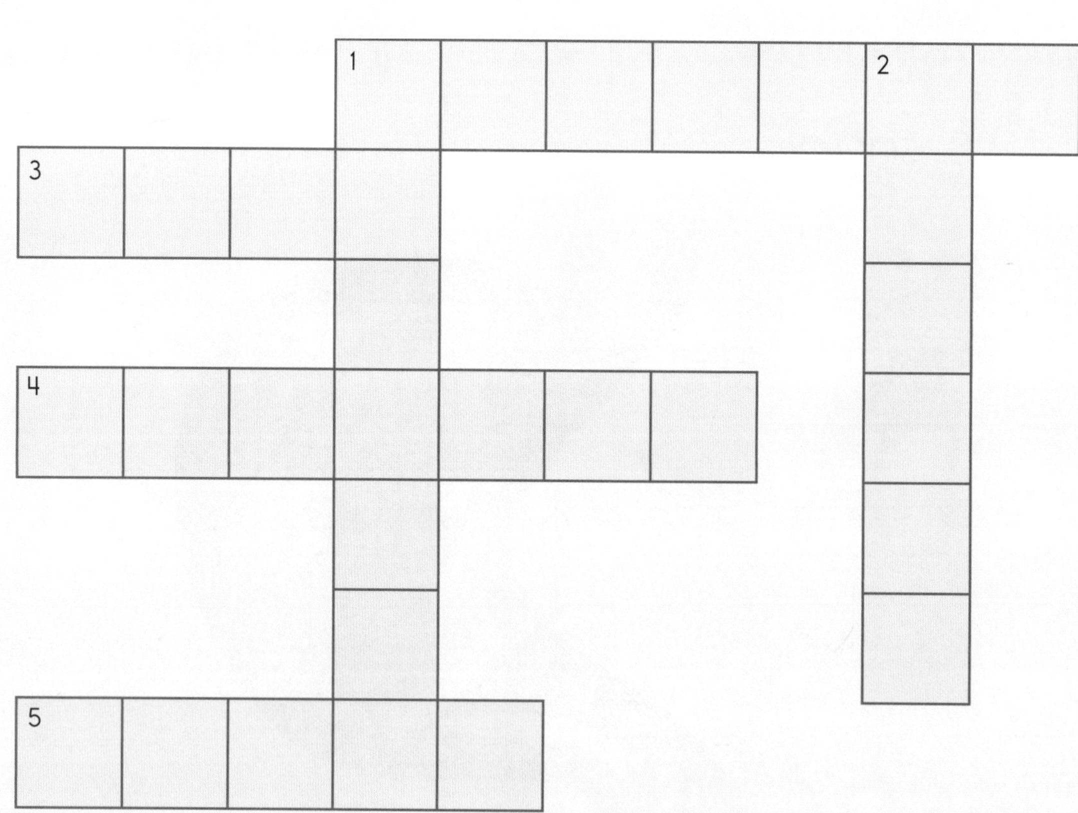

Word Pictures

COLOR the spaces that show words for **parts of the body**.

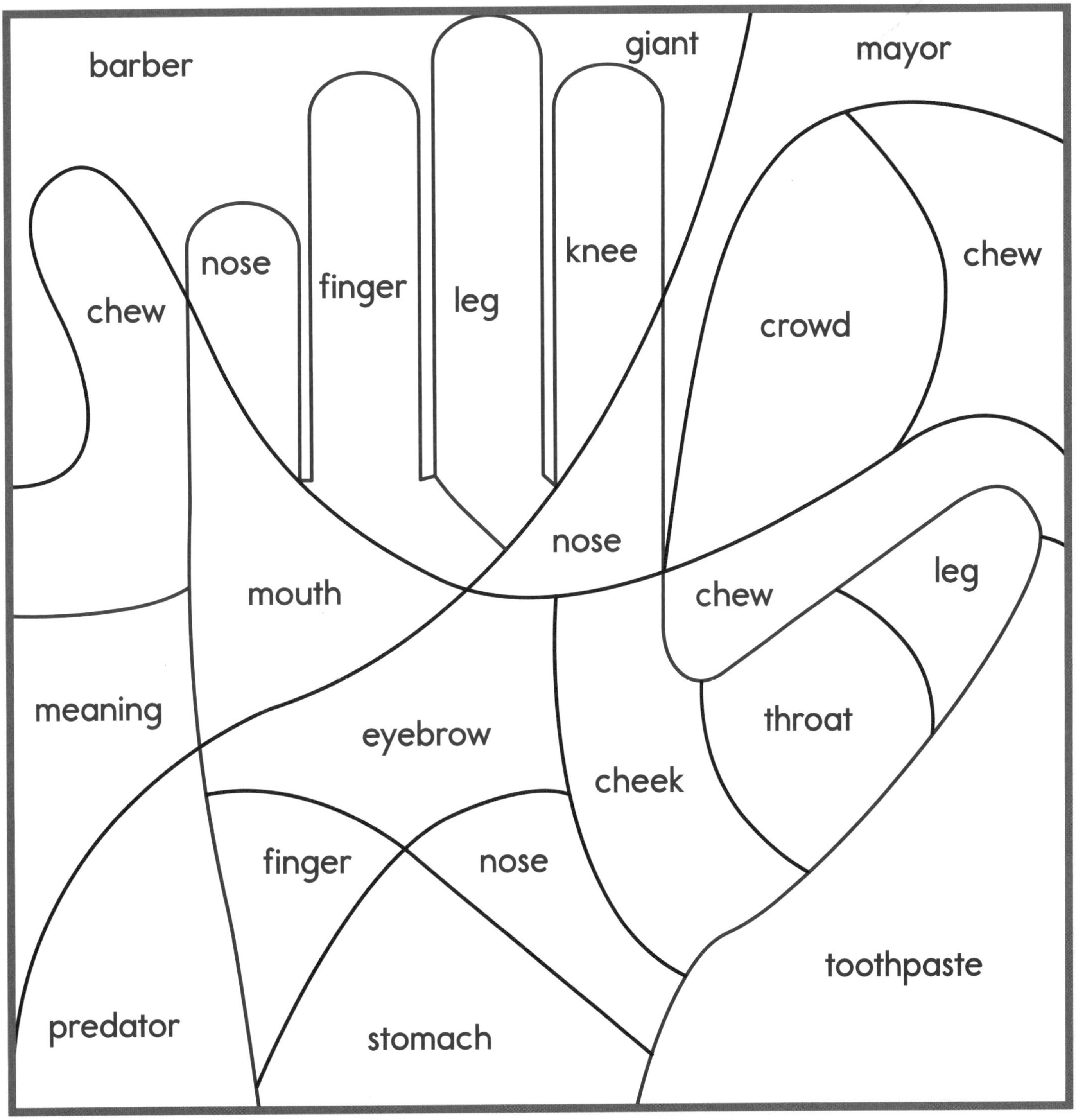

barber
giant
mayor
nose
finger
leg
knee
chew
chew
crowd
nose
mouth
chew
leg
meaning
eyebrow
throat
cheek
finger
nose
toothpaste
predator
stomach

Word List

READ the words and their meanings.

aunt—ant 1. *noun* the sister of your mother or father 2. *noun* the wife of your uncle

broth•er—BRUH*TH*-er *noun* a boy whose mother and father have another child

grand•fa•ther—GRAND-fah-*ther* 1. *noun* the father of your father or mother 2. *noun* your grandmother's husband

grand•moth•er—GRAND-muh*th*-er 1. *noun* the mother of your father or mother 2. *noun* your grandfather's wife

hus•band—HUHZ-buhnd *noun* a man who is married

sis•ter—SIHS-ter *noun* a girl whose mother and father have another child

un•cle—UHNG-kuhl 1. *noun* the brother of your mother or father 2. *noun* the husband of your aunt

wife—wif *noun* a woman who is married

Match the Meaning

WRITE the words next to their definitions. LOOK at the word box for help.

aunt	husband	brother	sister
grandfather	uncle	grandmother	wife

1. ______________ a man who is married
2. ______________ your grandmother's husband
3. ______________ another child (girl) of your parents
4. ______________ your aunt's husband
5. ______________ a woman who is married
6. ______________ another child (boy) of your parents
7. ______________ your uncle's wife
8. ______________ your grandfather's wife

Criss Cross

READ the clues. FILL IN the boxes with the right word for each clue.

HINT: You might have to look up some words in the clues.

Across

2. Your parent's father
3. A male spouse

Down

1. A male sibling

1

2

3

What do these words mean?

parent ______________________

sibling ______________________

spouse ______________________

Blank Out

FILL IN the blanks for each part of the family tree with the words in the word box. Use each word just once.

aunt	brother	grandfather	husband
uncle	sister	grandmother	wife

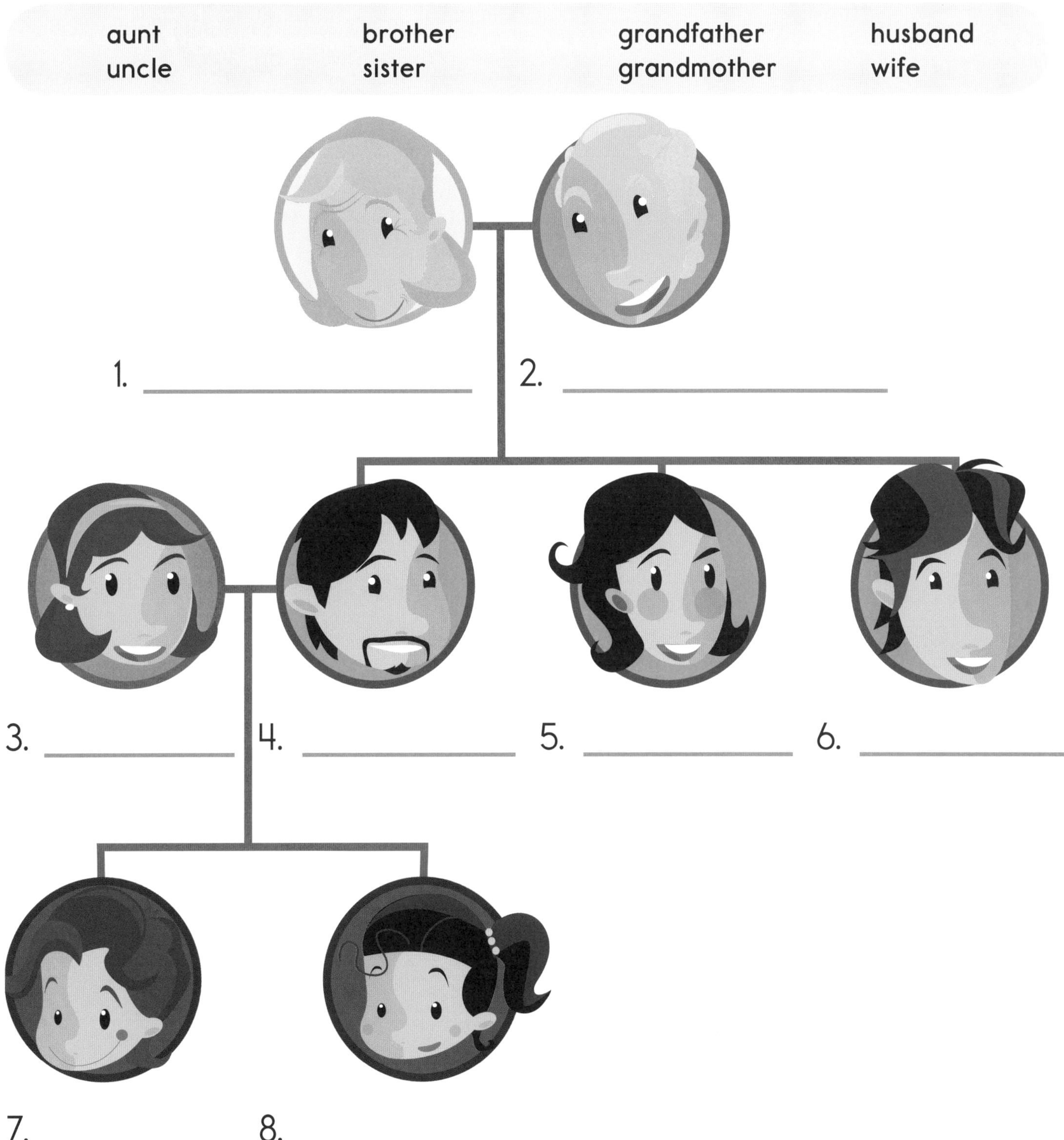

Right or Wrong?

UNDERLINE the sentence that matches the picture.

1.

Jen is Peter's brother.

Jen is Peter's sister.

2.

Stan is Sheila's husband.

Stan is Sheila's wife.

3.

Greg is Karl's grandfather.

Karl is Greg's grandfather.

4.

This is my uncle.

This is my aunt.

Cross Out

CROSS OUT the words that do **not** name family members.

1. grandfather	daughter	frighten	frown
2. son	bathroom	suggest	sister
3. predator	agree	mother	aunt
4. respect	uncle	brother	elephant

Word List

READ the words and their meanings.

base•ment—BAS-muhnt *noun* a room or rooms under a house or building

clos•et—CLAHZ-iht *noun* a very small room to keep clothes and shoes

com•fort•a•ble—KUHM-fer-tuh-buhl 1. *adjective* very soft or easy 2. *adjective* with no pain or fear

emp•ty—EHMP-tee *adjective* having nothing inside

fa•vor•ite—FA-ver-iht *adjective* the one that is liked the most

lawn—lawn *noun* the grass around a house

paint—peynt 1. *noun* color that can be put on walls or objects 2. *verb* to put color on something using paint

re•frig•er•a•tor—rih-FRIHJ-uh-ray-ter *noun* a metal box that keeps food and drinks cold

Match the Meaning

WRITE the words next to their definitions. LOOK at the word box for help.

basement	comfortable	favorite	paint
closet	empty	lawn	refrigerator

1. ____________________ the opposite of *full*
2. ____________________ a room just for coats and shoes
3. ____________________ the place under the house
4. ____________________ the one you like the best
5. ____________________ where you put food to keep it cold
6. ____________________ what makes the color on the walls
7. ____________________ nice and warm and soft
8. ____________________ a yard full of grass

Finish the Story

READ the story. FILL IN the blanks with words from the word box.

comfortable empty favorite lawn refrigerator

Bad Day

What a bad day! When I was hungry, the
_______________ was _______________.
1 2
There was nothing to eat! When I turned on the
TV, my _______________ show was over.
3
So I went to take a nap. Just when I got
_______________ on my bed, my brother started
4
to mow the _______________.
5
It was too loud to sleep!
I hope tomorrow is better.

Criss Cross

READ the clues. FILL IN the boxes with the right word for each clue.

Across

3. A room for clothes
4. Nothing inside
5. A grassy place

Down

1. Put color on walls
2. The lowest room

1
2
3
4
5

Right or Wrong?

UNDERLINE the sentence that matches the picture.

1.

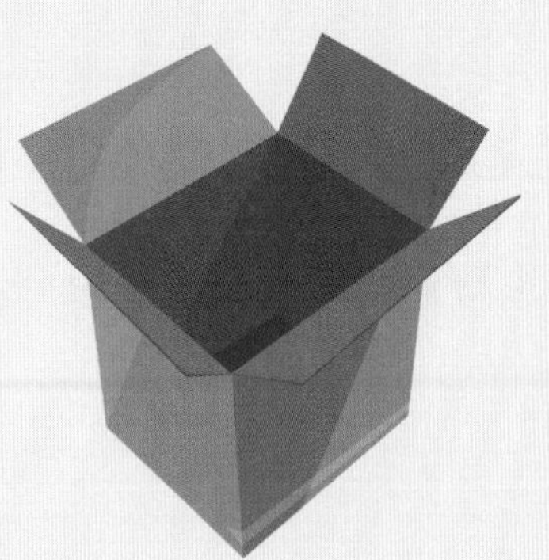

The box is empty.

The box is easy.

2.

The lawn is green.

The lane is green.

3.

That chair looks compatible.

That chair looks comfortable.

4.

That's Dipti's favorite doll.

That's Dipti's flavored doll.

Maze Crazy!

DRAW a line through the **adjectives** to get to the smiley face. Start at the yellow arrow.

Word List

READ the words and their meanings.

ba•nan•a—buh-NAN-uh *noun* a long, curved fruit with a yellow peel

bread—brehd *noun* a baked food made with flour that's used for toast and sandwiches

car•rot—KEHR-uht *noun* a skinny orange vegetable that grows underground

fruit—froot 1. *noun* a food that can be juicy and sweet, like an apple 2. *noun* the part of a plant that holds the seeds

spread—sprehd 1. *verb* to put something all over, like jam on bread 2. *verb* to open wide

stuffed—stuhft *adjective* filled with something, like a pillow is filled with fluff, or a belly is filled with food

taste—tayst 1. *noun* the way a food is salty, sweet, or icky 2. *verb* to put a bit of food in your mouth to see if you like it

veg•e•ta•ble—VEHJ-tuh-buhl *noun* a food that comes from a plant's leaves or roots

Match the Meaning

WRITE the words next to their definitions. LOOK at the word box for help.

banana	carrot	spread	taste
bread	fruit	stuffed	vegetable

1. ____________________ to try a bite of food
2. ____________________ an orange vegetable
3. ____________________ a fruit with a yellow peel
4. ____________________ the leaves or roots of a plant that you can eat
5. ____________________ very full of something
6. ____________________ part of the plant that has seeds
7. ____________________ to put something all over
8. ____________________ food that turns into toast

Find the Friend

READ the clues. Then WRITE the friend's name under each picture.

Shama is eating a fruit.

Mai has bananas on her shirt.

Crispin is eating vegetables.

Val has carrots on her shirt.

Lyle is eating bread.

Who am I?

1	2	3	4	5

Dictionary Dare

LOOK UP these foods in a dictionary. Then CIRCLE if it's a fruit or a vegetable.

1. **potato** fruit vegetable
2. **spinach** fruit vegetable
3. **cherry** fruit vegetable
4. **pear** fruit vegetable
5. **lettuce** fruit vegetable
6. **broccoli** fruit vegetable
7. **peach** fruit vegetable
8. **onion** fruit vegetable

Blank Out

FINISH each sentence with a word from the word box.

banana	carrots	spread	taste
bread	fruit	stuffed	vegetables

1. Cartoon rabbits are always chomping on ______________.
2. I love fish sticks, but Amy hates the way they ______________.
3. Nadine helped Mom ______________ frosting on the cake.
4. Isaac ate nothing but ______________ and butter all day.
5. A tomato is really a ______________ because it has seeds.
6. We were all ______________ after Thanksgiving dinner.
7. Chloe peeled the ______________ for the monkey to eat.
8. Saul eats his meat, but no leafy ______________.

Word Pictures

COLOR the spaces that show words for **food** and **eating**.

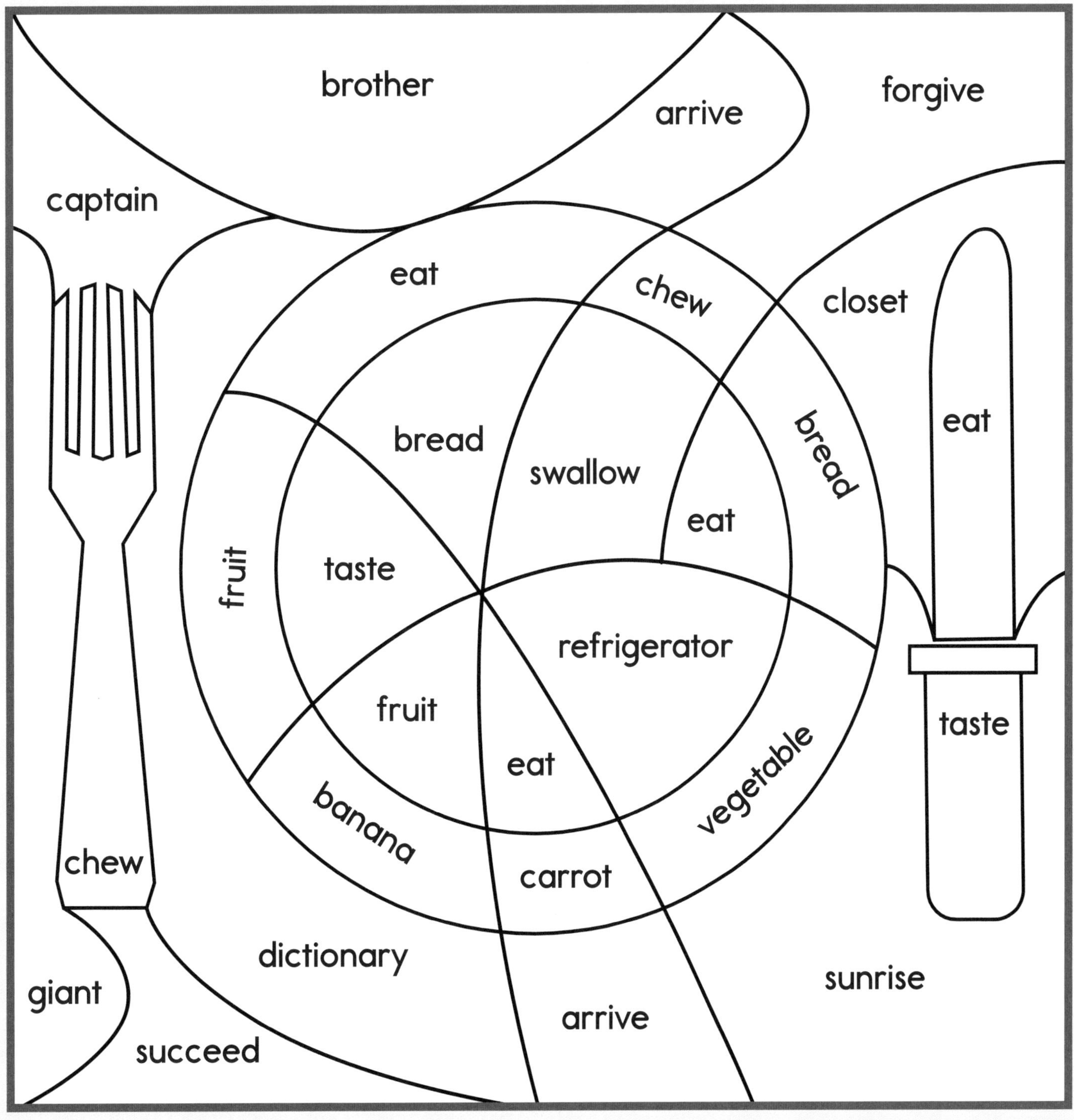

Pick the One

CIRCLE the correct part of speech for each word.

1. **freckles**	adjective	noun	verb
2. **sidewalk**	adjective	noun	verb
3. **favorite**	adjective	noun	verb
4. **agree**	adjective	noun	verb
5. **carrot**	adjective	noun	verb
6. **suggest**	adjective	noun	verb
7. **comfortable**	adjective	noun	verb
8. **fail**	adjective	noun	verb

Criss Cross

READ the clues. FILL IN the boxes with the right word for each clue.

enemy freckles frown spread teen uncle

Across

3. Spots on your skin
6. Not an adult or a child

Down

1. Your mother's brother
2. The opposite of *smile*
4. Put jam on bread
5. The opposite of *friend*

Cross Out

CROSS OUT the words that have more than two syllables.

1. beautiful	empty	braid	comfortable
2. predator	enemy	bathroom	toothpaste
3. meaning	adjective	freckles	everywhere
4. grandmother	throat	definition	lighthouse

Dictionary Dare

LOOK UP the words in a dictionary. Then WRITE the word from the word box that means the same thing.

actor	explain	frighten	taste
comfortable	forgive	frown	teen

1. pardon ____________
2. flavor ____________
3. grimace ____________
4. terrify ____________
5. adolescent ____________
6. thespian ____________
7. clarify ____________
8. snug ____________

Did you know that you can also use a book called a *thesaurus* to see a list of words that mean the same thing?

Word List

READ the words and their meanings.

beast—beest *noun* an animal or other creature that is not human and doesn't act human

crea·ture—KREE-cher *noun* a living animal or human

feath·er—FEH*TH*-er *noun* one of the soft pieces that cover a bird's body and wings

flight—flit 1. *noun* a trip through the air, like on a plane 2. *noun* a fast getaway, escape

flock—flahk 1. *noun* a group of birds 2. *verb* to make a group, like a flock of birds

herd—herd 1. *noun* a group of land animals like cows 2. *verb* to make a group of animals go somewhere

tame—taym 1. *adjective* quiet, safe, and nice 2. *verb* to make a wild animal be nice to humans

wild—wild 1. *adjective* not tame, not safe, not able to live with humans 2. *noun* a place where people don't live, like the jungle

Match the Meaning

WRITE the words next to their definitions. LOOK at the word box for help.

beast	feather	flock	tame
creature	flight	herd	wild

1. ____________________ a group of birds
2. ____________________ unsafe, not tame
3. ____________________ a creature that isn't human
4. ____________________ an air trip
5. ____________________ a human or an animal
6. ____________________ not a danger
7. ____________________ what you pluck from a bird
8. ____________________ a bunch of cows

Finish the Story

READ the story. FILL IN the blanks with words from the word box.

beasts	feathers	flocks	herds	tame	wild

A Trip to Africa

Africa is home to many _____________, like lions.
1

They're cats, but not like the _____________ kitties
2

we have in our homes. Lions are _____________
3

predators that may kill humans. In the skies above

Africa, you can see _____________ of beautiful
4

birds with colorful _____________. You might also
5

find giant _____________
6

of elephants walking for miles to find water.

Criss Cross

READ the clues. FILL IN the boxes with the right word for each clue.

Across

1. Birds that fly together
3. A crowd of cows
4. A sky trip

Down

2. A living being
4. It's on a bird's wing

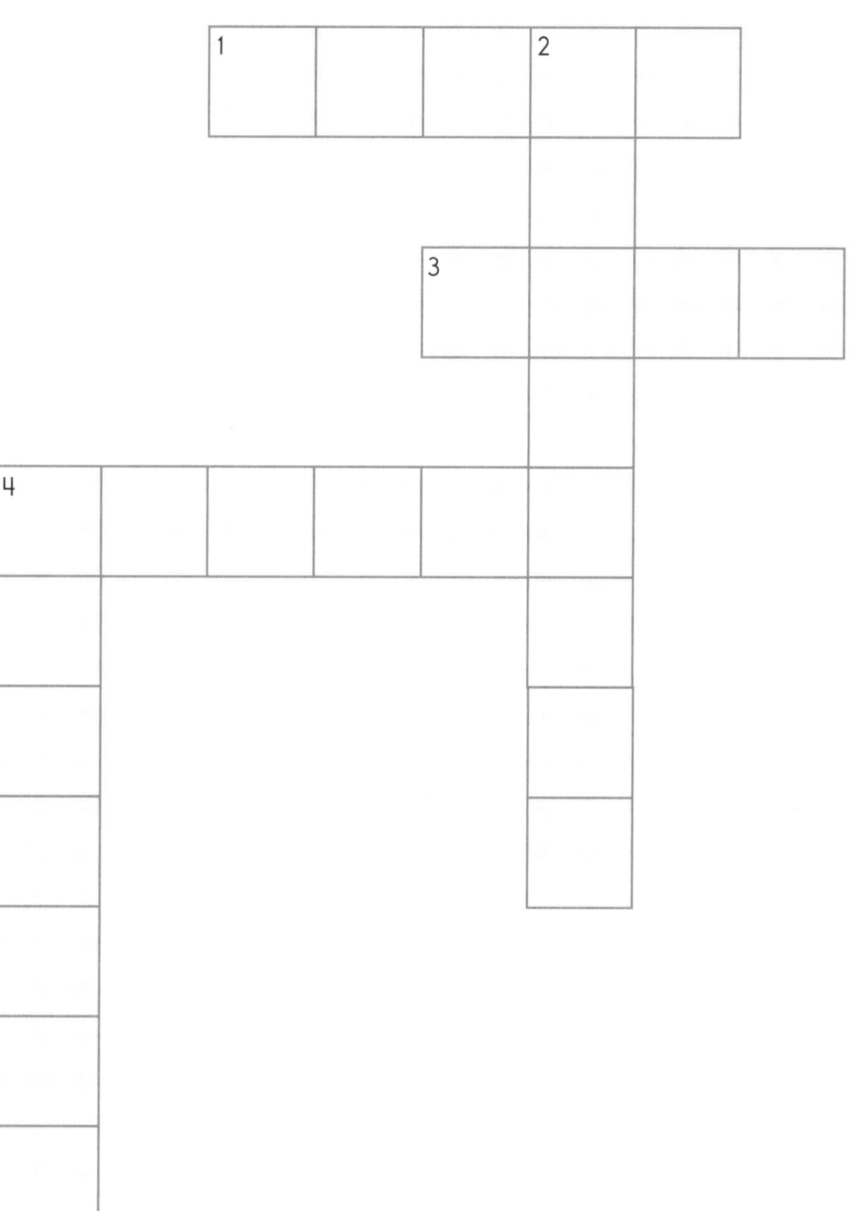

Right or Wrong?

UNDERLINE the sentence that matches the picture.

1.

A herd of geese flew by.

A flock of geese flew by.

2.

Mr. Tibbles is tame.

Mr. Tibbles is wild.

3.

This bird has green fathers.

This bird has green feathers.

4.

We are in the wild.

We are in the wind.

Word Pictures

COLOR the spaces that show words for **parts of animals**.

HINT: Don't forget to look up any words you don't know.

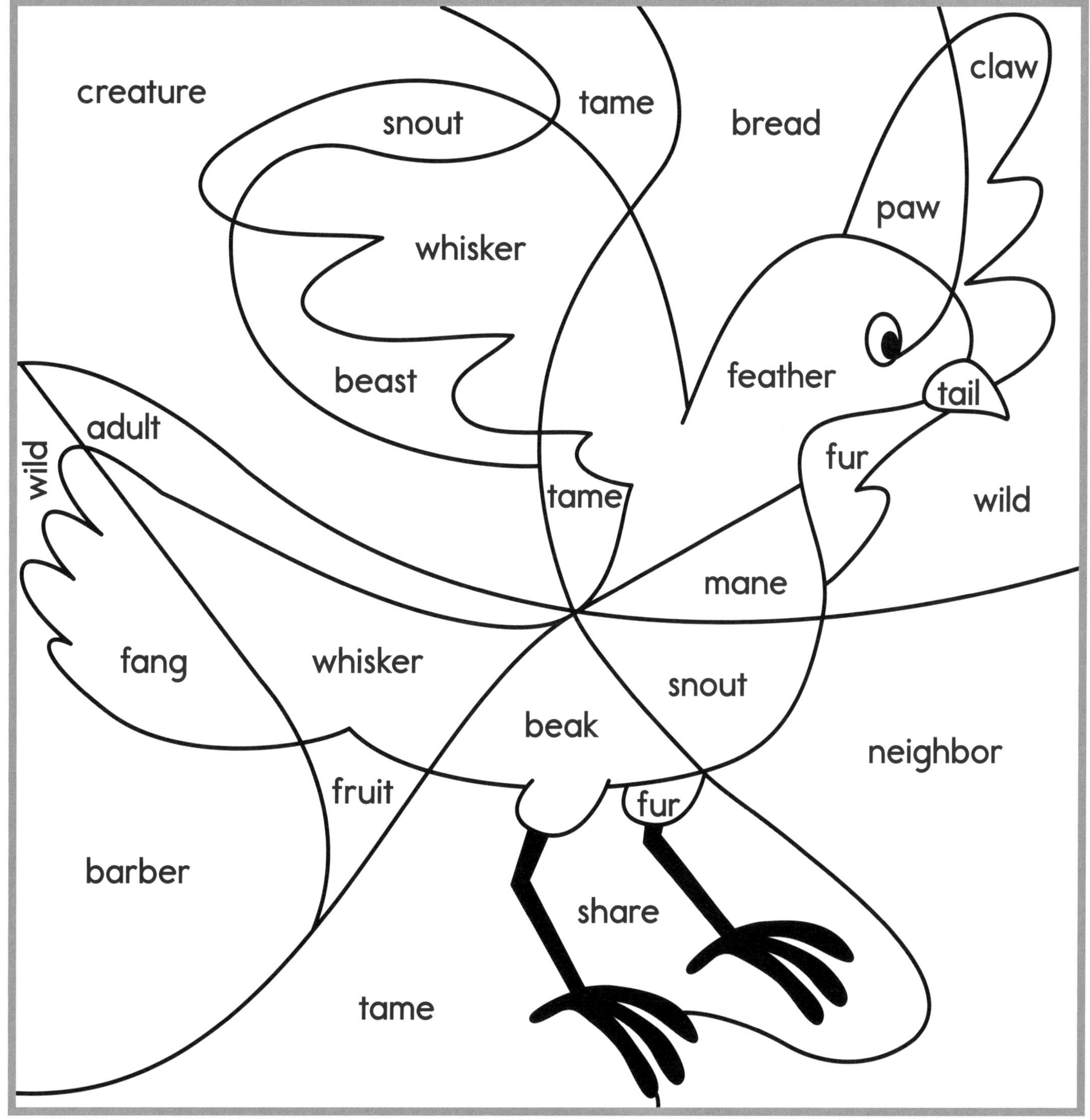

Word List

READ the words and their meanings.

an·ten·nae—an-TEHN-ee *noun* two thin feelers that help a bug sense the world

but·ter·fly—BUHT-er-fli *noun* an insect with large wings that are sometimes very colorful

cat·er·pil·lar—KAT-er-pihl-er *noun* an insect like a worm that turns into a butterfly or a moth

co·coon—kuh-KOON *noun* a silk wrap or bag made by an insect to keep its body or eggs safe. A caterpillar goes into a cocoon while turning into a moth.

hive—hiv *noun* a nest of bees, where they make honey

in·sect—IHN-sehkt *noun* a small creature with no backbone (a bug)

lar·va—LAHR-vuh *noun* a baby insect that looks like a worm. A caterpillar is the larva of a butterfly.

sting—stihng 1. *noun* the feeling of a bug bite or pin prick 2. *verb* to use a stinger or other sharp object to break someone's skin

Match the Meaning

WRITE the words in the box next to their definitions.

antennae	caterpillar	hive	larva
butterfly	cocoon	insect	sting

1. ____________________ a safe, silky wrap
2. ____________________ a bug
3. ____________________ feelers
4. ____________________ the larva of a moth or butterfly
5. ____________________ a sharp pain
6. ____________________ an insect with big wings
7. ____________________ a baby bug
8. ____________________ where bees live

Find the Friend

READ the clues. Then WRITE the friend's name under each picture.

Binky is in a cocoon.

Slinky is a caterpillar.

Tinky lives in a hive.

Pinky is a butterfly.

Dinky has purple antennae.

Who am I?

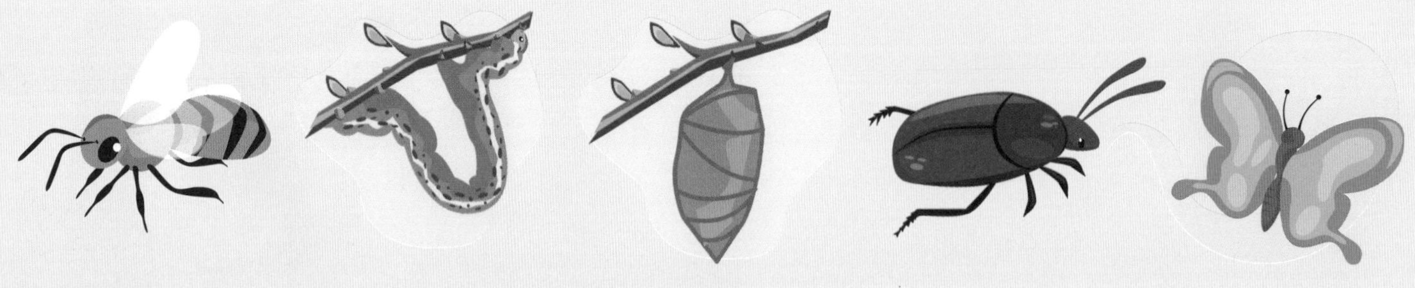

________ 1 ________ 2 ________ 3 ________ 4 ________ 5

Blank Out

FINISH each sentence with a word from the word box.

antennae	caterpillars	hives	larva
butterflies	cocoon	insects	sting

1. My arm still hurts from that bee ______________.
2. Some bugs use their ______________ to smell.
3. Teejay draws ______________ with giant, beautiful wings.
4. That wormy maggot is the ______________ of a fly.
5. Bears get honey from bee ______________ they find in the trees.
6. Some insects put their eggs in a ______________ to keep them safe.
7. I don't kill ______________ because one day they'll be butterflies!
8. Nate loves nature, but he hates ______________ that bite.

Criss Cross

READ the clues. FILL IN the boxes with the right word for each clue.

Across

2. A bug
5. A bug's feelers
6. A nest of bees

Down

1. A sharp pain
3. A safe, silky place
4. A baby bug

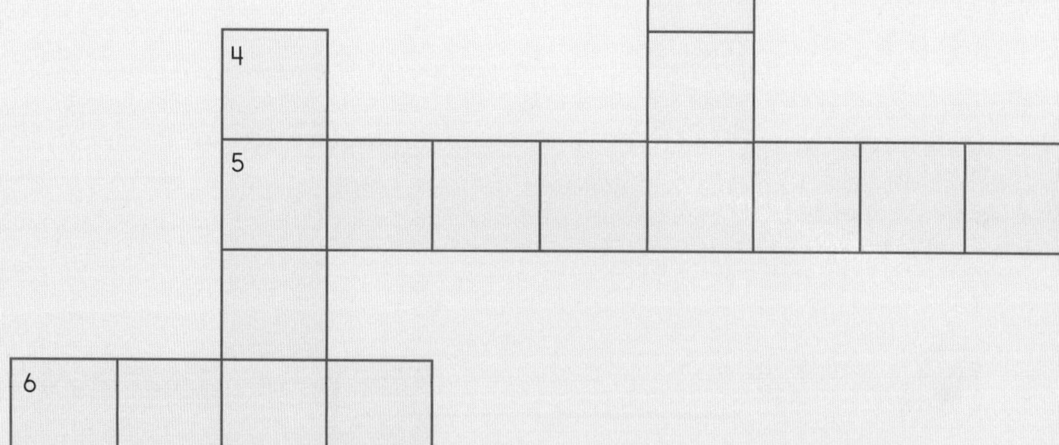

Maze Crazy!

DRAW a line through the words about **bugs** to get to the beehive.

Start at the green arrow.

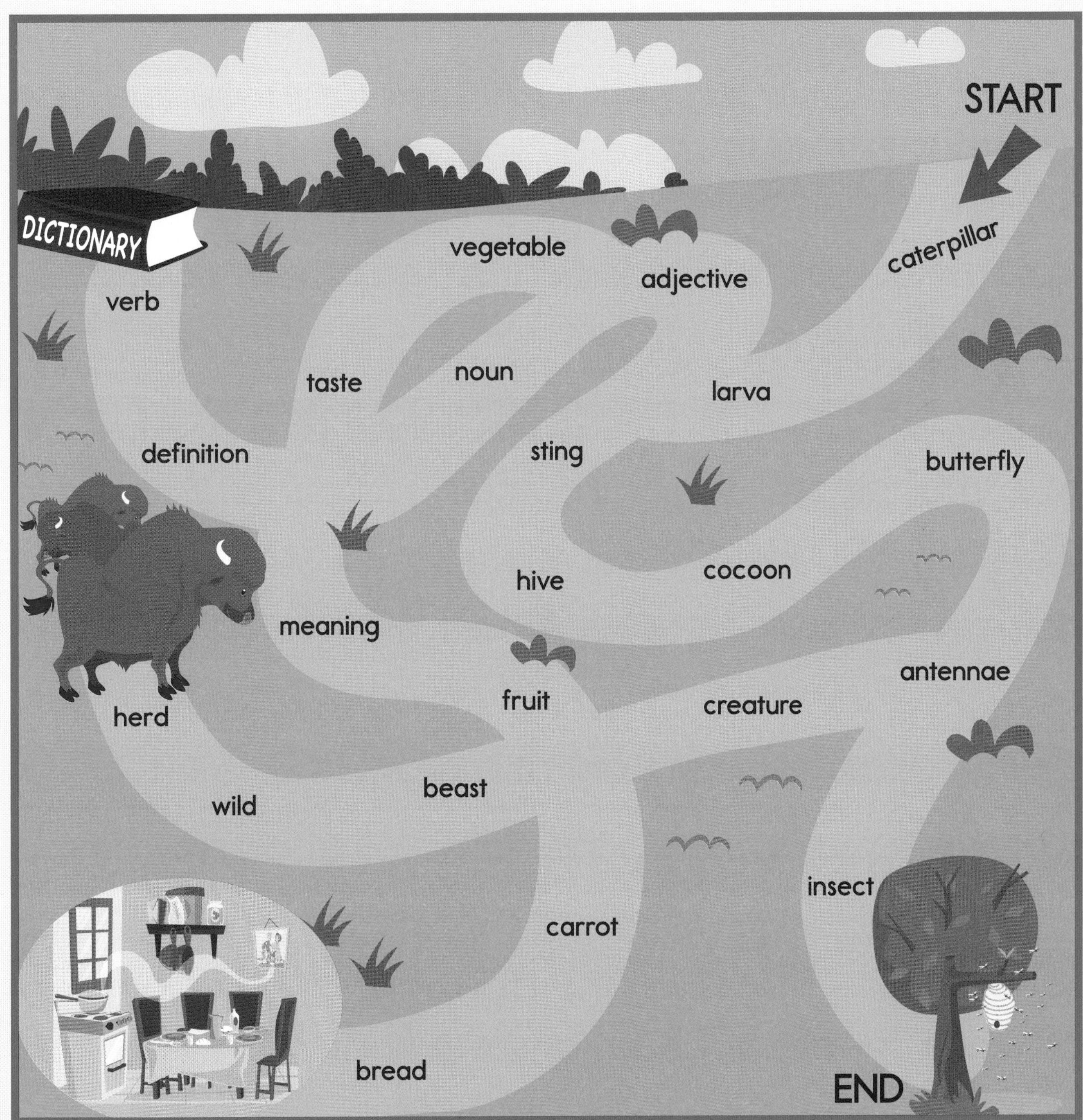

Word List

READ the words and their meanings.

chirp—cherp 1. *noun* the short, pretty sound a small bird makes 2. *verb* to make a chirping sound

click—klihk 1. *noun* a quick sound like teeth tapping together 2. *verb* to make a clicking sound

croak—krohk 1. *noun* the rough, deep sound of a frog, or your voice when your throat is sore 2. *verb* to make a croaking sound

jin•gle—JIHNG-guhl 1. *noun* the sound of a little bell, or two small pieces of metal bumping together 2. *verb* to make a jingling sound

nois•y—NOY-zee *adjective* loud, full of sound

speech—speech 1. *noun* words said by a person 2. *noun* a talk made in front of a crowd

squawk—skwahk 1. *noun* the noisy yell of a crow or other loud bird 2. *verb* to make a squawking sound

squeak—skweek 1. *noun* the high, tiny sound of a mouse, or when sneakers rub on a wood floor 2. *verb* to make a squeaking sound

Match the Meaning

WRITE the words next to their definitions. LOOK at the word box for help.

click	croak	noisy	squawk
chirp	jingle	speech	squeak

1. ____________________ loud
2. ____________________ the sound a little bird makes
3. ____________________ a high, tiny sound
4. ____________________ a sound like teeth tapping together
5. ____________________ the sound of a shaking bell
6. ____________________ words said out loud
7. ____________________ the yell of a loud bird
8. ____________________ the sound of a frog

Criss Cross

READ the clues. FILL IN the boxes with the right word for each clue.

Across

3. Your teeth can make this sound.
5. Full of sound
6. A mousy sound

Down

1. A sudden bird yell
2. Sounds like a tiny bell
4. A deep frog sound

Blank Out

FINISH each sentence with a word from the word box.

clicking	croak	noisy	squawks
chirping	jingle	speech	squeaking

1. Ben had a bad cold, so his voice sounded like a ________________.
2. The crowd was talking and clapping. It was very ________________.
3. Jess says we have mice. She hears them ________________ in the walls.
4. Mom gave a long, boring ________________ about doing chores.
5. I shivered so hard, my teeth were ________________ together.
6. Dad likes to ________________ his keys while he walks to the car.
7. The big parrot always ________________ when I come into the pet shop.
8. It was a nice morning. The sun was shining and the birds were ________________.

Pick the One

CIRCLE the sound that fits best for each word.

1. lion	roar	squeak	speech
2. dog toy	crash	bark	squeak
3. car horn	bang	honk	buzz
4. carrot	chirp	squeak	crunch
5. crow	squawk	roar	bark
6. push button	shout	quack	click
7. bird	bark	chirp	roar
8. frog	speech	croak	squeak

Cross Out

CROSS OUT the words that are **not** sounds.

1. click	carrot	larva	hoot
2. paint	teen	roar	squawk
3. honk	chirp	taste	kneel
4. squeak	cheek	screech	frown

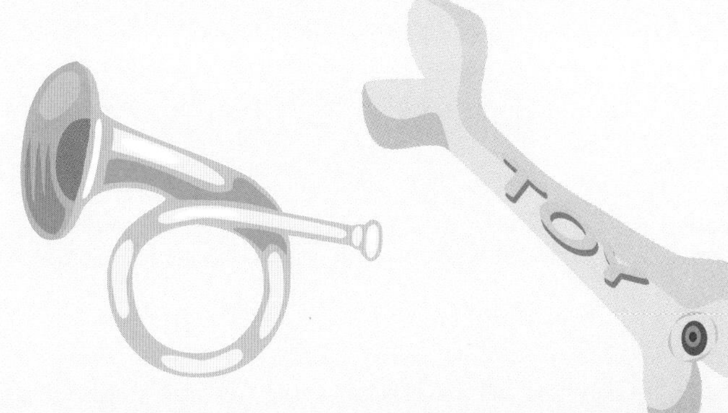

Blank Out

READ each word. Then WRITE the number of syllables in the blank.

HINT: Some of these have more syllables than you might think!

1. antennae ____________
2. cocoon ____________
3. caterpillar ____________
4. everywhere ____________
5. exercise ____________
6. favorite ____________
7. squawk ____________
8. taste ____________

Don't forget—a dictionary will show you the syllable breaks.

Same or Opposite?

READ each word pair. CIRCLE if they are the same or opposites.

1. squeak	roar	same	opposite
2. wild	tame	same	opposite
3. stuffed	full	same	opposite
4. noisy	quiet	same	opposite
5. speak	talk	same	opposite
6. beast	animal	same	opposite
7. borrow	return	same	opposite
8. insect	bug	same	opposite

Criss Cross

WRITE the word for each clue in the grids.

agree captain exercise respect share speech

Across

1. Give to others
2. What you do at the gym
3. Leader of the team
5. Honor someone

Down

1. All talk
4. Say yes

Dictionary Dare

READ the guide words. CIRCLE the word in each row that comes between them.

1. **commercial → communicate**

   commentary commodity community

2. **whippoorwill → whiten**

   whisper whinny whittle

3. **shoelace → shortening**

   shovel shoal shoplifter

4. **guard → guillotine**

   guacamole gullible guidance

5. **mischief → missile**

   misunderstand miser misuse

6. **insolent → instrument**

   insulin inspire insight

7. **referendum → refugee**

   reforest referee refund

8. **presently → president**

   presence preserve presume

Word List

READ the words and their meanings.

crop—krahp *noun* a planting of something, like corn, that a farmer is growing in a field

field—feeld *noun* a wide space of ground that has plants growing in it, like grass or a crop

flood—fluhd 1. *noun* a lot of water that overflows from a river, or fills an area like a house 2. *verb* to fill an area with water

moun•tain—MOWN-tuhn *noun* a tall peak of land, much higher than a hill

nat•u•ral—NATCH-er-uhl 1. *adjective* the way nature made it, not changed by humans 2. *adjective* not fake

shade—shad *noun* a place where the sun is blocked by something, like under a tree

soil—soyl 1. *noun* dirt that is used for growing plants 2. *verb* to make something dirty

val•ley—VAL-ee *noun* a low spot between hills or mountains

Match the Meaning

WRITE the words in the box next to their definitions.

crop	flood	natural	soil
field	mountain	shade	valley

1. ____________ a really tall hill
2. ____________ a cool, dark spot
3. ____________ a bunch of plants, like corn
4. ____________ a low spot between hills
5. ____________ a place to grow crops
6. ____________ not changed
7. ____________ a lot of water
8. ____________ dirt

Blank Out!

FINISH each sentence with a word from the box.

crops	flooded	natural	soiled
field	mountain	shade	valley

1. The plastic tree in the living room doesn't look ____________.
2. Next to our house is a big ____________ full of weeds.
3. On a hot day, it's nice to sit in the ____________ of a tree.
4. We live in a deep ____________ that follows a river.
5. After Zan walked in the mud, his socks were all ____________.
6. Farmer Ned grows three ____________: corn, wheat, and oats.
7. Last year, my Uncle Jaime climbed a tall ____________.
8. We had to stay in a hotel because our house ____________ in the storm.

Right or Wrong?

UNDERLINE the sentence that matches the picture.

1. 

Vernon is sitting in the shake.

Vernon is sitting in the shade.

2. 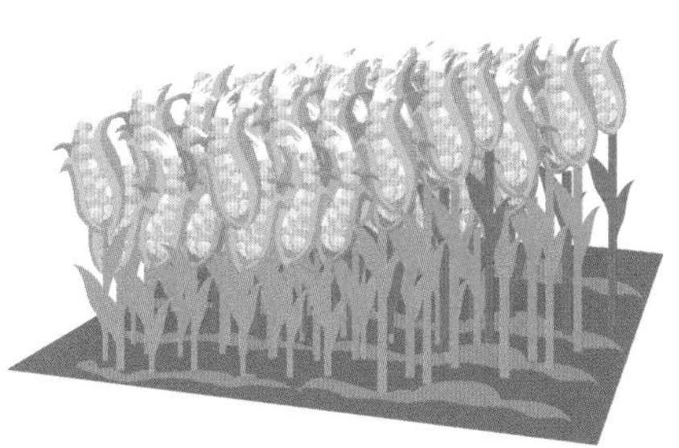

Corn is growing in this field.

Corn is growing in this feel.

3. 

This soil is good for growing things.

This soap is good for growing things.

4. 

The house is on the mountain.

The house is in the valley.

Same or Opposite?

READ each word pair. CIRCLE if they are the same or opposites.

HINT: Look up any words you don't know.

1. mountain	valley	same	opposite
2. fake	natural	same	opposite
3. soil	dirt	same	opposite
4. field	meadow	same	opposite
5. natural	unchanged	same	opposite
6. flooded	dry	same	opposite
7. soiled	clean	same	opposite
8. shady	sunny	same	opposite

Word Pictures

COLOR the spaces that show words for things in nature.

HINT: Don't forget to look up any words you don't know.

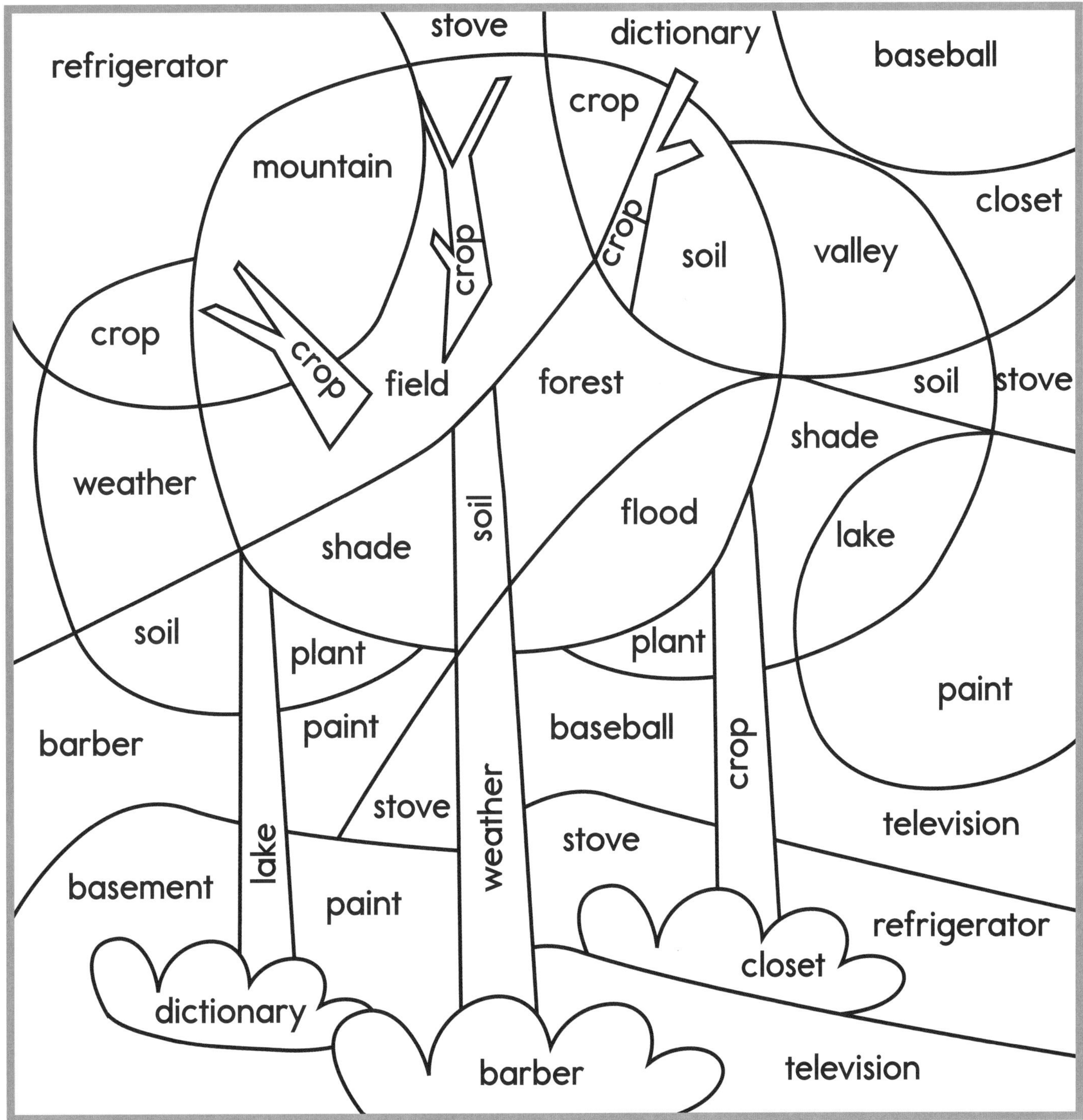

Word List

READ the words and their meanings.

el•e•va•tor—EHL-uh-vay-ter *noun* a moving box that takes you up to the high floors of a building

lit•ter—LIHT-er 1. *noun* trash that is on the ground 2. *verb* to leave trash on the ground

lone•ly—LOHN-lee *adjective* sad because there's nobody around

mod•ern—MAHD-dern *adjective* very new and up to date, not old

mon•u•ment—MAHN-yuh-muhnt *noun* anything that is put up to honor a person or event

neigh•bor•hood—NAY-ber-hud *noun* an area where people live

rude—rood *adjective* not nice, makes other people feel bad

spend—spehnd *verb* to use up, like money or time

Match the Meaning

WRITE the words next to their definitions. LOOK at the word box for help.

elevator	lonely	monument	rude
litter	modern	neighborhood	spend

1. ____________________ the area where you live
2. ____________________ to leave trash on the street
3. ____________________ not old fashioned
4. ____________________ a box that takes you up
5. ____________________ to use up
6. ____________________ sad and alone
7. ____________________ something to honor a person
8. ____________________ not nice

Finish the Story

READ the story. FILL IN the blanks with words from the box.

elevator	modern	neighborhood	spend
lonely	monument	rude	

A New Friend

I get a little ______________ in the summer when all
1

the kids in my ______________ go to camp. I
2

______________ a lot of time playing at the park
3

by myself. There's a ______________ there, of a big,
4

stone soldier. One day, I saw a girl sitting on the soldier's foot. At first she was ______________ and
5

wouldn't talk to me. But now we hang out all the time! She lives in a new, ______________ apartment
6

building with an ______________ to take
7

you to her floor. I hope we stay friends when the summer is over!

Criss Cross

READ the clues. FILL IN the boxes with the right word for each clue.

HINT: Look up words you don't know.

Across

1. New
2. By yourself and sad
3. Lets you skip the stairs

Down

1. A statue that honors someone
2. Trash on the street

1
2
3

Word List

READ the words and their meanings.

back•ward—BAK-werd 1. *adverb* back in the direction you came from 2. *adjective* pointing the wrong way, so the front is facing back

coun•try—KUHN-tree 1. *noun* the nation where you live, like the United States or Canada 2. *noun* a place far away from any city, where there is more nature

di•rec•tion—duh-REHK-shuhn 1. *noun* the way you're going, like left or north 2. *noun* an order, like "go to bed now"

for•ward—FOR-werd *adverb* in a straight direction

is•land—I-luhnd *noun* a piece of land that is in the ocean, with water on all sides

lan•guage—LANG-gwihj *noun* the kind of speech used in different countries, like English or French

trav•el—TRAV-uhl 1. *noun* a visit to another place 2. *verb* to go somewhere

va•ca•tion—vay-KAY-shuhn 1. *noun* a break from work or school 2. *verb* to take a break, maybe travel

Match the Meaning

WRITE the words next to their definitions. LOOK at the word box for help.

backward	direction	island	travel
country	forward	language	vacation

1. ________________ like France or England
2. ________________ land with water all around
3. ________________ the opposite of *forward*
4. ________________ to take a trip
5. ________________ an order from someone
6. ________________ time off from work
7. ________________ keep going straight
8. ________________ what speech you use

Find the Friend

READ the clues. Then WRITE the friends' names next to the corresponding numbers.

Jorge lives in the country of France.

Chantal's shirt is backward.

Simon lives on an island.

Fiona is traveling.

Mona is on vacation in Germany.

Who am I?

1. ____________________
2. ____________________
3. ____________________
4. ____________________
5. ____________________

Blank Out

FINISH each sentence with a word from the word box.

backward	directions	islands	traveled
country	forward	language	vacation

1. In chorus, we have to face ____________ and smile at the crowd.
2. At our school, we get two months of ____________ in the summer.
3. I'm from India. What ____________ are you from?
4. Last year, my uncle ____________ all over the world!
5. People who look ____________ when they walk will bump into things.
6. Hawaii is a string of ____________.
7. North, south, east, and west are all ____________ on a map.
8. Sometimes I think my math teacher is speaking another ____________.

Right or Wrong?

UNDERLINE the sentence that matches the picture.

1.

Staci is walking forward.

Staci is walking backward.

2.

Martin is on an island.

Martin is on a mountain.

3.

Xyqx speaks a different langor.

Xyqx speaks a different language.

4.

Joel is in the country.

Joel is in the city.

Maze Crazy!

DRAW a line through words about **travel** to get to the train. Start at the green arrow.

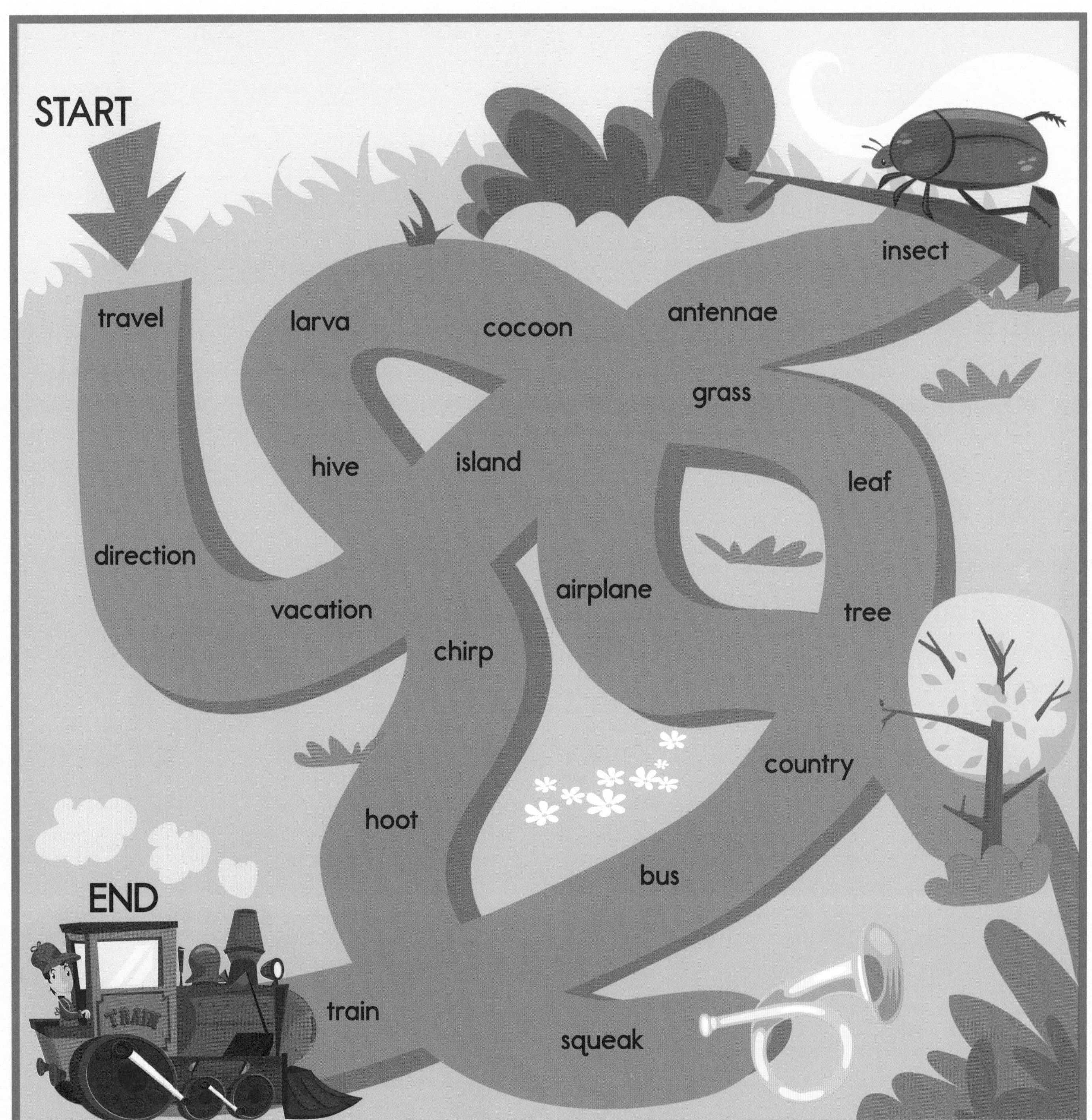

Dictionary Dare

LOOK UP the words in a dictionary. Then FILL IN the blanks with words from the box that mean the **opposite**.

agree	crowd	predator	stuffed
basement	noise	rude	tame

1. individual ________________
2. attic ________________
3. starving ________________
4. savage ________________
5. refuse ________________
6. prey ________________
7. polite ________________
8. silence ________________

Blank Out

FINISH each sentence with a word from the word box.

adjectives	country	dictionary	opposite
compound	definition	language	verb

1. Canada is a ________________.

2. *Pretty* and *purple* are ________________.

3. Every word has a ________________.

4. You can look up a word's meaning in the ________________.

5. A word that names an action is a ________________.

6. *Night* is the ________________ of *day*.

7. *Lighthouse* is a ________________ word.

8. English is a ________________.

Pick the One

READ each sentence. CIRCLE the correct part of speech for each word in green.

HINT: Some words are tricky because they can be nouns, verbs, or adjectives!

1. That man littered the sidewalk with his lunch bag.

   noun verb adjective

2. This is Gerri's second attempt at that skateboard trick.

   noun verb adjective

3. The door clicked as it slid open.

   noun verb adjective

4. Mom cried when she saw our flooded basement.

   noun verb adjective

5. Do you have time to braid my hair?

   noun verb adjective

6. All the kids flock around the ice cream truck when it comes.

   noun verb adjective

7. Can I have a taste of that cake?

   noun verb adjective

Cross Out

CROSS OUT the words that are **not** nouns.

1. comfortable	monument	forgive	toothpaste
2. flight	lonely	stomach	borrow
3. succeed	wife	basement	empty
4. arrive	elevator	rude	neighborhood

Index

ac•tor—AK-ter *noun* a person who acts on stage or screen

ad•jec•tive—AJ-ihk-tihv *noun* a word that describes something, like *pretty* or *blue*

a•dult—uh-DUHLT 1. *noun* a person who is grown up 2. *adjective* fully grown

a•gree—uh-GREE 1. *verb* to think the same way as someone else 2. *verb* to say yes to something

an•ten•nae—an-TEHN-ee *noun* two thin feelers that help a bug sense the world

ar•rive—uh-RIV *verb* to come to a place

at•tempt—uh-TEHMPT *verb* to try to do something

aunt—ant 1. *noun* the sister of your mother or father 2. *noun* the wife of your uncle

back•ward—BAK-werd 1. *adverb* back in the direction you came from 2. *adjective* pointing the wrong way, so the front is facing back

ba•nan•a—buh-NAN-uh *noun* a long, curved fruit with a yellow peel

bar•ber—BAHR-ber *noun* a person who cuts hair

base•ball—BAYS-bahl 1. *noun* a game played with a bat, a ball, and four bases 2. *noun* a ball used for playing baseball

base•ment—BAS-muhnt *noun* a room or rooms under a house or building

bath•room—BATH-room *noun* a room for bathing and using the toilet

beast—beest *noun* an animal or other creature that is not human and doesn't act human

beau•ti•ful—BYOO-tuh-fuhl *adjective* very pretty

bor•row—BAHR-oh *verb* when someone allows you to take something for a short time, then give it back

braid—brayd 1. *noun* hair in a rope-like style 2. *verb* to put hair in a rope-like style

bread—brehd *noun* a baked food made with flour that's used for toast and sandwiches

breathe—bree*th* *verb* to take in air through your mouth or nose

broth•er—BRUH*TH*-er *noun* a boy whose mother and father have another child

but•ter•fly—BUHT-er-fli *noun* an insect with large wings that are sometimes very colorful

cap•tain—KAP-tihn 1. *noun* the leader of a sports team 2. *noun* the leader of a ship or airplane 3. *noun* the leader of firefighters, police, or the military

car•rot—KEHR-uht *noun* a skinny orange vegetable that grows underground

cat•er•pil•lar—KAT-er-pihl-er *noun* an insect like a worm that turns into a butterfly or a moth

cheek—cheek *noun* the side of your face between your nose and your ear. You have two cheeks.

chew—choo *verb* to use your teeth to bite food in your mouth

chirp—cherp 1. *noun* the short, pretty sound a small bird makes 2. *verb* to make a chirping sound

click—klihk 1. *noun* a quick sound like teeth tapping together 2. *verb* to make a clicking sound

clos•et—CLAHZ-iht *noun* a very small room to keep clothes and shoes

co•coon—kuh-KOON *noun* a silk wrap or bag made by an insect to keep its body or eggs safe. A caterpillar goes into a cocoon while turning into a moth.

com•fort•a•ble—KUHM-fer-tuh-buhl 1. *adjective* very soft or easy, 2. *adjective* with no pain or fear

coun•try—KUHN-tree 1. *noun* the nation where you live, like the United States or Canada 2. *noun* a place far away from any city, where there is more nature

crea•ture—KREE-cher *noun* a living animal or human

croak—krohk 1. *noun* the rough, deep sound of a frog, or your voice when your throat is sore 2. *verb* to make a croaking sound

crop—krahp *noun* a planting of something, like corn, that a farmer is growing in a field

crowd—krowd *noun* a lot of people all together

def•i•ni•tion—dehf-uh-NIHSH-uhn *noun* the meaning of a word

de•scribe—dih-SKRIB *verb* to make a picture with words, like "a pretty girl in a blue dress"

dic•tion•ar•y—DIHK-shuh-nehr-ee *noun* a book filled with definitions of words

di•rec•tion—duh-REHK-shuhn 1. *noun* the way you're going, like left or north 2. *noun* an order, like "go to bed now"

el•e•va•tor—EHL-uh-vay-ter *noun* a moving box that takes you up to the high floors of a building

emp•ty—EHMP-tee *adjective* having nothing inside

en•e•my—EHN-uh-mee *noun* someone who is working against you, a foe

eve•ry•where—EHV-ree-wehr *adverb* in all places

ex•er•cise—EHK-ser-siz 1. *noun* a set of moves that work out your body 2. *noun* an activity that helps practice a lesson 3. *verb* to move your body to make it strong and fit

ex•plain—ihk-SPLAYN *verb* to tell or teach someone about something

eye•brow—I-brow *noun* the strip of hair above your eye

fail—fayl *verb* to lose, to not get what you tried for

fa•vor•ite—FA-ver-iht *adjective* the one that is liked the most

feath•er—FEH*TH*-er *noun* one of the soft pieces that cover a bird's body and wings

field—feeld *noun* a wide space of ground that has plants growing in it, like grass or a crop

flight—flit 1. *noun* a trip through the air, like on a plane 2. *noun* a fast getaway, escape

flock—flahk 1. *noun* a group of birds 2. *verb* to make a group, like a flock of birds

flood—fluhd 1. *noun* a lot of water that overflows from a river, or fills an area like a house 2. *verb* to fill an area with water

for•give—fer-GIHV *verb* to stop being mad and make up after a fight with someone

for•ward—FOR-werd *adverb* in a straight direction

freck•les—FREHK-lz *noun* spots on skin from the sun

fright•en—FRIT-uhn *verb* to scare somebody

frown—frown 1. *noun* a sad or mad face, the opposite of a smile 2. *verb* to make a sad or mad face

fruit—froot 1. *noun* a food that can be juicy and sweet, like an apple 2. *noun* the part of a plant that holds the seeds

gi•ant—JI-uhnt 1. *noun* a huge person or other creature out of a fairy tale 2. *adjective* very big

grand•fa•ther—GRAND-fah-*ther* 1. *noun* the father of your father or mother 2. *noun* your grandmother's husband

grand•moth•er—GRAND-muh*th*-er 1. *noun* the mother of your father or mother 2. *noun* your grandfather's wife

herd—herd 1. *noun* a group of land animals like cows 2. *verb* to make a group of animals go somewhere

hive—hiv *noun* a nest of bees, where they make honey

hus•band—HUHZ-buhnd *noun* a man who is married

in•sect—IHN-sehkt *noun* a small creature with no backbone (a bug)

is•land—I-luhnd *noun* a piece of land that is in the ocean, with water on all sides

jin•gle—JIHNG-guhl 1. *noun* the sound of a little bell, or two small pieces of metal bumping together 2. *verb* to make a jingling sound

kneel—neel *verb* to get down on your knees

lan•guage—LANG-gwihj *noun* the kind of speech used in different countries, like English or French

lar•va—LAHR-vuh *noun* a baby insect that looks like a worm. A caterpillar is the larva of a butterfly.

lawn—lawn *noun* the grass around a house

light•house—LIT-hows *noun* a tall building with a big light that helps boats see the shore

lit•ter—LIHT-er 1. *noun* trash that is on the ground 2. *verb* to leave trash on the ground

lone•ly—LOHN-lee *adjective* sad because there's nobody around

may•or—MAY-er *noun* the leader of a town or city

mean•ing—MEE-nihng *noun* the idea of a word, what it means

mod•ern—MAHD-dern *adjective* very new and up to date, not old

mon•u•ment—MAHN-yuh-muhnt *noun* anything that is put up to honor a person or event

moun•tain—MOWN-tuhn *noun* a tall peak of land, much higher than a hill

mouth—mowth 1. *noun* the hole in your face where you put your food 2. *verb* to talk with your lips without making a sound

nat•u•ral—NATCH-er-uhl 1. *adjective* the way nature made it, not changed by humans 2. *adjective* not fake

neigh•bor—NAY-ber *noun* a person who lives next door to or near you

neigh•bor•hood—NAY-ber-hud *noun* an area where people live

nois•y—NOY-zee *adjective* loud, full of sound

noun—nown *noun* a word that stands for a person, place, or thing

paint—peynt 1. *noun* color that can be put on walls or objects 2. *verb* to put color on something using paint

pred•a•tor—PREHD-uh-ter *noun* an animal or insect that hunts others for its food

reach—reech 1. *verb* to put out your hand to get something 2. *verb* to arrive at a place

re•frig•er•a•tor—rih-FRIHJ-uh-ray-ter *noun* a metal box that keeps food and drinks cold

re•spect—rih-SPEHKT 1. *noun* a feeling that you honor someone 2. *verb* to honor and show consideration for someone

rude—rood *adjective* not nice, makes other people feel bad

shade—shad *noun* a place where the sun is blocked by something, like under a tree

share—shehr 1. *noun* one person's part of something that can be split 2. *verb* to let other people use your things or eat your food 3. *verb* to use something with other people

shiv•er—SHIHV-er 1. *noun* a shake of the body 2. *verb* to shake your body, like when it's cold

side•walk—SID-wawk *noun* a smooth, hard walkway

sis•ter—SIHS-ter *noun* a girl whose mother and father have another child

skate—skayt 1. *noun* a shoe with a sharp blade that helps you slide on ice 2. *noun* a shoe with wheels that help you roll on the sidewalk 3. *verb* to use skates to move along the ground or on ice

soil—soyl 1. *noun* dirt that is used for growing plants 2. *verb* to make something dirty

speech—speech 1. *noun* words said by a person 2. *noun* a talk made in front of a crowd

spend—spehnd *verb* to use up, like money or time

spread—sprehd 1. *verb* to put something all over, like jam on bread 2. *verb* to open wide

squawk—skwahk 1. *noun* the noisy yell of a crow or other loud bird 2. *verb* to make a squawking sound

squeak—skweek 1. *noun* the high, tiny sound of a mouse, or when sneakers rub on a wood floor 2. *verb* to make a squeaking sound

squirm—skwerm *verb* to move around in a twisty-turny way

sting—stihng 1. *noun* the feeling of a bug bite or pin prick 2. *verb* to use a stinger or other sharp object to break someone's skin

stom•ach—STUHM-uhk *noun* your tummy, or belly, that tells you when you're hungry or full

stop•light—STAHP-lit *noun* a light that helps move traffic safely where two roads cross

stuffed—stuhft *adjective* filled with something, like a pillow is filled with fluff, or a belly is filled with food

suc•ceed—suhk-SEED *verb* to win, to get what you wanted

sug•gest—suhg-JEHST 1. *verb* to hint at something 2. *verb* to give an idea or plan as an option

sun•rise—SUHN-riz *noun* the time of day when the sun comes up

swal•low—SWAHL-oh *verb* to let food go from your mouth into your throat and stomach

tame—taym 1. *adjective* quiet, safe, and nice 2. *verb* to make a wild animal be nice to humans

taste—tayst 1. *noun* the way a food is salty, sweet, or icky 2. *verb* to put a bit of food in your mouth to see if you like it

teen—teen *noun* a person who is older than a child but younger than an adult

throat—throht 1. *noun* the front part of your neck 2. *noun* the tube inside your neck that goes to your stomach and your lungs

tooth•paste—TOOTH-payst *noun* a cream used to clean teeth

trav•el—TRAV-uhl 1. *noun* a visit to another place 2. *verb* to go somewhere

un•cle—UHNG-kuhl *noun* 1. the brother of your mother or father 2. *noun* the husband of your aunt

va•ca•tion—vay-KAY-shuhn 1. *noun* a break from work or school 2. *verb* to take a break, maybe travel

val•ley—VAL-ee *noun* a low spot between hills or mountains

veg•e•ta•ble—VEHJ-tuh-buhl *noun* a food that comes from a plant's leaves or roots

verb—verb *noun* a word that stands for an action, like *run*

wife—wif *noun* a woman who is married

wild—wild 1. *adjective* not tame, not safe, not able to live with humans 2. *noun* a place where people don't live, like the jungle

Answers

Page 3
1. describe
2. meaning
3. verb
4. noun
5. adjective
6. dictionary
7. definition

Page 4
1. angry
2. balloon
3. jelly
4. learn
5. machine
6. octopus
7. trouble
8. whisper

Page 5
1. verb
2. adjective
3. verb
4. noun
5. adjective
6. verb
7. noun
8. noun

Page 6
1. food
2. present
3. traffic
4. rock
5. bagpipes
6. monarch
7. unique
8. hawk

Page 7
1. 3
2. 4
3. 2
4. 4
5. 2
6. 1
7. 3
8. 1

Page 9
1. giant
2. fail
3. succeed
4. predator
5. arrive
6. beautiful
7. attempt
8. enemy

Page 10
1. opposite
2. same
3. opposite
4. opposite
5. same
6. same
7. opposite
8. same

Page 11
1. Kira
2. Joe
3. Larry
4. Darla
5. Talia

Page 12

ACROSS	DOWN
2. arrive	1. beautiful
4. giant	3. enemy
5. fail	

Page 13
1. 3
2. NO
3. **Suggestion:** I don't skate very well.

Page 15
1. everywhere
2. sunrise
3. baseball
4. sidewalk
5. lighthouse
6. toothpaste
7. bathroom
8. stoplight

Page 16
1. sunrise
2. baseball
3. toothpaste
4. bathroom
5. sidewalk
6. stoplight

Page 17
1. grand + father = grandfather
2. skate + board = skateboard
3. play + ground = playground
4. news + paper = newspaper
5. green + house = greenhouse

Page 18

sunrise → sunset
troublemaker → peacemaker
somebody → nobody
downstairs → upstairs
nighttime → daytime
everything → nothing
bedtime → playtime
highway → sidewalk

Page 19
1. starfish, football, ~~adjective,~~ ~~predator~~
2. ~~enemy,~~ playground, everybody, ~~arrive~~
3. lighthouse, ~~beautiful,~~ ~~dictionary,~~ blueberry
4. stoplight, ~~unhappy,~~ nothing, ~~syllable~~

Page 20
1. adjective
2. arrive
3. attempt
4. definition
5. describe
6. dictionary
7. sidewalk
8. stoplight

Page 21
1. adjective
2. noun
3. verb
4. noun
5. verb
6. adjective
7. verb
8. noun

Page 22
1. opposite
2. same
3. same
4. opposite
5. same
6. same
7. opposite
8. opposite

Page 23

ACROSS	DOWN
3. succeed	1. describe
4. verb	2. adjective
	3. syllable

Page 25
1. frown
2. throat
3. mouth
4. braid
5. freckles
6. eyebrow
7. stomach
8. cheek

Page 26

ACROSS	DOWN
3. throat	1. frown
5. cheek	2. stomach
	4. freckles

Page 27
1. finger, throat, ~~verb,~~ ~~definition~~
2. ~~sunrise,~~ ~~fail,~~ freckles, mouth
3. arm, ~~sidewalk~~, stomach, ~~attempt~~
4. ~~syllable,~~ eyebrow, ~~giant~~, cheek

Page 28
1. Tyara
2. Connor
3. Carly
4. Jordan
5. Doug

Page 29
1. cheek
2. mouth
3. stomach
4. eyebrow
5. freckles
6. throat

Page 31
1. squirm
2. kneel
3. shiver
4. chew
5. swallow
6. reach
7. breathe
8. exercise

Page 32
1. Maddy is chewing gum.
2. Mr. Santos is exercising.
3. Ty kneels on the ground.
4. The baby reaches for her bottle.

Page 33
1. shiver
2. exercise
3. reach
4. squirming
5. swallow
6. kneel
7. chew
8. breathe

Page 34
1. squirm
2. breathe
3. beautiful
4. reach
5. shiver
6. swallow
7. chew
8. enemy

Page 35

Page 37
1. teen
2. adult
3. crowd
4. actor
5. barber
6. mayor
7. captain
8. neighbor

Page 38
1. crowd
2. mayor
3. captain
4. actor
5. barber
6. neighbor

Answers

Page 39

ACROSS	DOWN
2. teen	1. neighbor
4. adult	3. mayor
5. barber	

Page 40
1. Leena
2. Serena
3. Hunter
4. Cyrus
5. Bart

Page 41

Page 43
1. respect
2. share
3. borrow
4. explain
5. suggest
6. agree
7. frighten
8. forgive

Page 44
1. Tom does not respect Donna.
2. Jean shares her pizza with Mike.
3. Sondra frightens Neal.
4. Neal forgives Sondra.

Page 45
1. borrow
2. explain
3. respect
4. beautiful
5. share
6. neighbor
7. enemy
8. agree

Page 46
1. explain
2. forgive
3. respect
4. suggests
5. agree
6. shares
7. frighten
8. borrow

Page 47
1. ~~enemy~~, ~~beautiful~~, forgive, attempt
2. frighten, ~~scary~~, exercise, ~~definition~~
3. ~~verb~~, share, ~~throat~~, borrow
4. respect, ~~sidewalk~~, suggest, ~~idea~~

Page 48
1. ginger
2. outsmart
3. spindle
4. aunt
5. country
6. north
7. wear
8. incomplete

Page 49
1. scare → frighten
2. succeed → win
3. hunter → predator
4. try → attempt
5. meaning → definition
6. come → arrive
7. tummy → stomach
8. shake → shiver

Page 50

ACROSS	DOWN
1. suggest	1. swallow
3. chew	2. squirm
4. explain	
5. crowd	

Page 51

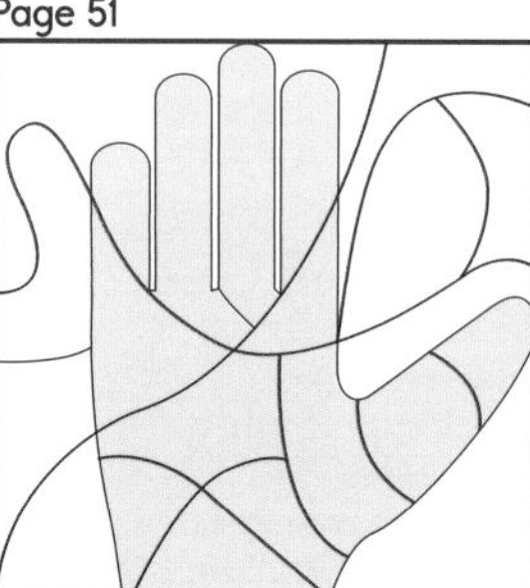

Page 53
1. husband
2. grandfather
3. sister
4. uncle
5. wife
6. brother
7. aunt
8. grandmother

Page 54

ACROSS	DOWN
2. grandfather	1. brother
3. husband	

parent: a mother or father
sibling: a brother or sister
spouse: a husband or wife

Page 55
1. grandmother
2. grandfather
3. wife
4. husband
5. aunt
6. uncle
7. brother
8. sister

Page 56
1. Jen is Peter's sister.
2. Stan is Sheila's husband.
3. Greg is Karl's grandfather.
4. This is my aunt.

Page 57
1. grandfather, daughter, ~~frighten~~, ~~frown~~
2. son, ~~bathroom~~, ~~suggest~~, sister
3. ~~predator~~, ~~agree~~, mother, aunt
4. ~~respect~~, uncle, brother, ~~elephant~~

Page 59
1. empty
2. closet
3. basement
4. favorite
5. refrigerator
6. paint
7. comfortable
8. lawn

Page 60
1. refrigerator
2. empty
3. favorite
4. comfortable
5. lawn

Page 61

ACROSS	DOWN
3. closet	1. paint
4. empty	2. basement
5. lawn	

Page 62
1. The box is empty.
2. The lawn is green.
3. That chair looks comfortable.
4. That's Dipti's favorite doll.

Page 63

Page 65
1. taste
2. carrot
3. banana
4. vegetable
5. stuffed
6. fruit
7. spread
8. bread

Page 66
1. Crispin
2. Lyle
3. Shama
4. Mai
5. Val

Page 67
1. vegetable
2. vegetable
3. fruit
4. fruit
5. vegetable
6. vegetable
7. fruit
8. vegetable

Page 68
1. carrots
2. taste
3. spread
4. bread
5. fruit
6. stuffed
7. banana
8. vegetables

Page 69

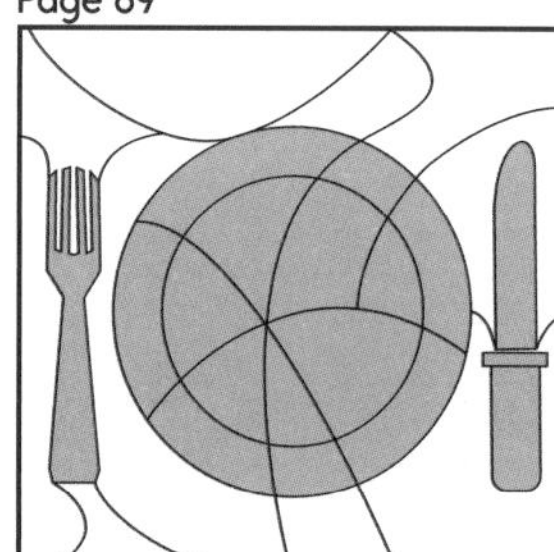

Page 70
1. noun
2. noun
3. adjective
4. verb
5. noun
6. verb
7. adjective
8. verb

Page 71

ACROSS	DOWN
3. freckles	1. uncle
6. teen	2. frown
	4. spread
	5. enemy

Answers

Page 72

1. ~~beautiful~~, empty, braid, ~~comfortable~~
2. ~~predator~~, ~~enemy~~, bathroom, toothpaste
3. meaning, ~~adjective~~, freckles, ~~everywhere~~
4. ~~grandmother~~, throat, ~~definition~~, lighthouse

Page 73

1. forgive
2. taste
3. frown
4. frighten
5. teen
6. actor
7. explain
8. comfortable

Page 75

1. flock
2. wild
3. beast
4. flight
5. creature
6. tame
7. feather
8. herd

Page 76

1. beasts
2. tame
3. wild
4. flocks
5. feathers
6. herds

Page 77

ACROSS	DOWN
1. flock	2. creature
3. herd	4. feather
4. flight	

Page 78

1. A flock of geese flew by.
2. Mr. Tibbles is tame.
3. This bird has green feathers.
4. We are in the wild.

Page 79

Page 81

1. cocoon
2. insect
3. antennae
4. caterpillar
5. sting
6. butterfly
7. larva
8. hive

Page 82

1. Tinky
2. Slinky
3. Binky
4. Dinky
5. Pinky

Page 83

1. sting
2. antennae
3. butterflies
4. larva
5. hives
6. cocoon
7. caterpillars
8. insects

Page 84

ACROSS	DOWN
2. insect	1. sting
5. antennae	3. cocoon
6. hive	4. larva

Page 85

Page 87

1. noisy
2. chirp
3. squeak
4. click
5. jingle
6. speech
7. squawk
8. croak

Page 88

ACROSS	DOWN
3. click	1. squawk
5. noisy	2. jingle
6. squeak	4. croak

Page 89

1. croak
2. noisy
3. squeaking
4. speech
5. clicking
6. jingle
7. squawks
8. chirping

Page 90

1. roar
2. squeak
3. honk
4. crunch
5. squawk
6. click
7. chirp
8. croak

Page 91

1. click, ~~carrot~~, ~~larva~~, hoot
2. ~~paint~~, ~~teen~~, roar, squawk
3. honk, chirp, ~~taste~~, ~~kneel~~
4. squeak, ~~cheek~~, screech, ~~frown~~

Page 92

1. 3
2. 2
3. 4
4. 3
5. 3
6. 3
7. 1
8. 1

Page 93

1. opposite
2. opposite
3. same
4. opposite
5. same
6. same
7. opposite
8. same

Page 94

ACROSS	DOWN
1. share	1. speech
2. exercise	4. agree
3. captain	
5. respect	

Page 95

1. commodity
2. whisper
3. shoplifter
4. guidance
5. miser
6. inspire
7. reforest
8. preserve

Page 97

1. mountain
2. shade
3. crop
4. valley
5. field
6. natural
7. flood
8. soil

Page 98

1. natural
2. field
3. shade
4. valley
5. soiled
6. crops
7. mountain
8. flooded

Page 99

1. Vernon is sitting in the shade.
2. Corn is growing in this field.
3. This soil is good for growing things.
4. The house is in the valley.

Page 100

1. opposite
2. opposite
3. same
4. same
5. same
6. opposite
7. opposite
8. opposite

Page 101

Page 103

1. neighborhood
2. litter
3. modern
4. elevator
5. spend
6. lonely
7. monument
8. rude

Page 104

1. lonely
2. neighborhood
3. spend
4. monument
5. rude
6. modern
7. elevator

Page 105

ACROSS	DOWN
1. modern	1. monument
2. lonely	2. litter
3. elevator	

Answers

Page 107
1. country
2. island
3. backward
4. travel
5. direction
6. vacation
7. forward
8. language

Page 108
1. Fiona
2. Chantal
3. Jorge
4. Mona
5. Simon

Page 109
1. forward
2. vacation
3. country
4. traveled
5. backward
6. islands
7. directions
8. language

Page 110
1. Staci is walking forward.
2. Martin is on a mountain.
3. Xyqx speaks a different language.
4. Joel is in the country.

Page 111

Page 112
1. crowd
2. basement
3. stuffed
4. tame
5. agree
6. predator
7. rude
8. noise

Page 113
1. country
2. adjectives
3. definition
4. dictionary
5. verb
6. opposite
7. compound
8. language

Page 114
1. verb
2. noun
3. verb
4. adjective
5. verb
6. verb
7. noun

Page 115
1. ~~comfortable~~, monument, ~~forgive~~, toothpaste
2. flight, ~~lonely~~, stomach, ~~borrow~~
3. ~~succeed~~, wife, basement, ~~empty~~
4. ~~arrive~~, elevator, ~~rude~~, neighborhood